Millennials in Ministry

Blessings as you serve the Kingdom! Jolene Erlacher

Jolene Cassellius Erlacher

Foreword by Molly T. Marshall

JUDSON PRESS
PUBLISHERS SINCE 1824

Join our mailing list for updates and special offers.
www.judsonpress.com/mailing_list.cfm

*To my parents and siblings, for teaching me
about loving and serving God*

*To Matthew, for supporting and pursuing
God's calling on our lives*

Millennials in Ministry
© 2014 by Judson Press, Valley Forge, PA 19482-0851
All rights reserved.

Interior design by Beth Oberholtzer.
Cover design by Thom Fecik.

Library of Congress Cataloging-in-Publication data

Erlacher, Jolene Cassellius.
    Millennials in ministry / Jolene Cassellius Erlacher. — first [edition].
        pages   cm
    ISBN 978-0-8170-1752-1 (pbk. : alk. paper) 1. Church work with young adults. 2. Generation Y. 3. Christian leadership. I. Title.
    BV4446.E75 2014
    262'.140842—dc23

                                                                2014008418

Printed in the U.S.A.
First printing, 2014.

Contents

CONTENTS

PART IV
Practical Applications

Foreword

"Where have all the young folks gone?" At the risk of sounding like a holdover from the 1960s, this refrain is often heard in our congregations. It is also the lament of many leadership teams who have not been able to retain Millennials in their staff configurations. What is it about this generation that creates some uneasy tension with churches, nonprofits, mission agencies, and other institutional expressions of ministry?

Jolene Cassellius Erlacher offers the reader a map for navigating constructive relationships with these born between 1980 and 1995. With appreciative insight, she probes the distinctive formation and characteristics of this generation. She also invites Millennials to overhear the conversation and reflect with those Silent, Boomer, and Gen X generations about how to live into gospel values together.

Rather than expressing impatience with Millennials, which these other generations often do, the author sees the promise of their giftedness and commitments for the work of the Reign of God. Their desire for authenticity in relationships is the key ingredient to their vocations, a desire which is instructional for all.

An underlying theme in the book is the providence of God in calling persons uniquely equipped for new horizons in ministry. Millennials, of course, are products of contemporary culture, but they also are able to pierce the surface to interpret the holy longings at work in forms of communication, art, and improvisatory communities. Listening to these emerging voices is essential for the mission of God to continue.

The author reminds us that Millennials have little patience with institutional commitments that are not transformative for the real needs of people. Facilities, budgets, and programs—deliverables by which most churches and agencies measure themselves—may be superfluous over against the goal of "doing life together," as one Millennial leader put it. They desire a compelling vision for their ministry and want to participate where real change can occur.

The book provides some sage wisdom for those who would create space for leadership development for Millennials. Listen to their stories of calling; disclose something of your own narrative; be accessible; respect their deep connectedness with family and friends; do not quash their earnest desire to change the world; keep at bay jaded cynicism; and encourage them to experiment, granting Millennial leaders real authority for implementation.

The concluding section of the book is all about practical implications for generational collaboration in ministry. The author's thesis comes into full view with these words: "Failure to invest in Millennials and prepare them for effective and enduring leadership deprives the kingdom of God of leaders desperately needed to guide churches and organizations through tumultuous times ahead." The reader gets the sense that this is a beloved cohort for the author—essential for constructive perspective.

Cultivating this significant generation for present and future leadership will bear good fruit, the kind that endures. Learning to become "Millennial-friendly" is all about Christian hospitality; it is also about transgressing boundaries that would otherwise render the gospel inaccessible. Readers will find clear navigational instruments for this shared journey in these pages.

Molly T. Marshall

President, Central Baptist Theological Seminary

Acknowledgments

I would like to take this opportunity to thank those whose example, perspectives, and support made this project possible: the students, staff, faculty, and administration at North Central University, who first inspired my interest in this topic; the faculty in the Leadership, Policy, and Administration program at the University of St. Thomas, for their encouragement and advice as I began this research; my editor, Rebecca Irwin-Diehl, who has believed in this project and provided insightful feedback; the inspiring young adults in ministry roles who took the time to share their experiences, dreams, and perspectives with me; the friends and colleagues who read and responded to portions of this project; my family and friends who provided endless encouragement and help as I researched and wrote as a busy new mommy of beautiful twin girls; and most importantly, my Savior, who lovingly pursues every generation with grace and truth . . . may he be glorified above all.

Introduction

"Why are so many young graduates of seminary and ministry programs working as baristas at Starbucks, doing freelance work, or starting their own businesses after short stints in ministry positions?" This question initiated my research journey several years ago into the topic of Millennials in ministry. I started reading every book and article I could find on the topic of Millennials. As I did so, I began to realize much had been written about Millennials in the corporate workplace, and some research had been conducted regarding the perspectives of Millennials in general regarding the church. However, regarding the unique population of students I saw at the Christian university where I worked, almost no discussion existed.

The students I interacted with daily felt called to serve God, the kingdom, and the church in some capacity. For some that entailed vocational church work; for others it meant pursuing education, missions, community development, or international relief work. These young people came to us excited, passionate, and inspired. After four years of preparation, they went out to put into practice their hopes and ideas. I watched as many of them left their ministry positions within a few years, returned home from places of service, and in some cases, abandoned their faith altogether. These were not nominal believers, but rather young adults who desired to dedicate their lives to service, ministry, and advancing the kingdom of God. In other cases, young adults remained in their positions, but lost their passion and excitement.

Then, in a few notable situations, I saw our Millennial alumni thriving in ministry work. These cases piqued my curiosity to learn what made the difference for them. How could we—as leaders of schools, churches, missions agencies, and nonprofit organizations—effectively develop, correct, and empower the next generation of leaders? What fate awaited the church if future pastors and leaders, those called to serve, ended up disillusioned, burnt-out, or lacking in the character and skills needed for ministry within a decade of their high school graduations? These questions drove my pursuit of understanding a new generation of leaders entering ministry.

After several years of reading as much as I could on the subject of Millennials; of presenting on and interacting around the topic in various venues with pastors, ministry leaders, and educators; and of mentoring and teaching Millennials preparing for and serving in ministry for almost a decade, I decided to conduct an in-depth qualitative study to answer the questions that kept emerging. The goal of my research was to understand what factors contributed to the job satisfaction and retention of Millennials serving in churches and other ministry settings.

Over the course of two-and-a-half years, I conducted in-depth interviews with over thirty Millennials who had served or were serving in ministry positions. All of the participants in my research were born between 1980 and 1990. They were between the ages of 22 and 32 at the time of the interviews. These young people represented ten different denominations and missions agencies, and served in ten different states and five different countries. Some were in extremely rural settings, others in the inner-city of large metropolitan areas. Church and organization sizes ranged from 30 to 4,500 members. Ministry experiences included children, youth, and family work; music and worship ministry; senior pastoring; adult ministries; teaching; administration; prayer ministry; missions; and community and relief work. Length of time in ministry positions ranged from three months to more than six years. Those interviewed who no longer served in ministry had worked for a minimum of nine months in a ministry position prior to changing vocations. Most participants had attended a Christian college, university, or seminary, and the majority had degrees in ministry or theology-related topics.

So, why is this research important? Understanding and relating to individuals whose worldview, preferences, and expectations differ from our own is difficult and often results in frustration, miscommunication, and pain. Generations working together today encounter dissimilarities with the potential to produce significant misunderstandings, dysfunction, and disunity. Effective and fulfilling intergenerational relationships require personal sacrifice, humility, patience, and love from all involved. I am convinced that the Holy Spirit has instilled in every generation the tools, perspectives, and passion needed in a particular season to propel the kingdom of God forward. I also believe there are forces at work that would undermine God's purpose and seek to corrupt characteristics, gifts, and vision that God has ordained for each generation. Older generations possess a sacred responsibility to recognize God's work, and we are entrusted with teaching, correcting, coaching, and empowering those who will follow us. Deuteronomy 4:9 (NIV) challenges us, "Watch yourselves closely so that you do not forget the things your eyes have seen or let them fade from your heart as long as you live. Teach them to your children and to their children after them."

This book is written to those leaders, mentors, teachers, and supervisors who desire to understand, empower, encourage, and mentor individuals in the Millennial generation who are called to ministry, those who will lead in the years to come. Millennials possess a number of characteristics that have potential to concern, exasperate, and exhaust those with years of faithful ministry experience. Some of the statements and stories in this book may even produce disbelief, scorn, or derision. I respectfully ask you to suspend judgment and endeavor to hear the heart of this generation. They did not raise themselves, and many of their weaknesses result from parenting styles, social systems, and cultural beliefs we allowed, and at times facilitated. I hope the research and the conclusions presented in the following pages offer hope, practical perspectives, strategies, and insights to help us as we seek to understand and engage this emerging generation of leaders effectively.

To Millennials reading this book, I commend you for taking the time to understand your own generation better. May you be encouraged by the heart of your generation, and challenged to overcome obstacles and weaknesses that threaten your ministry effectiveness. Because of the diversity inherent in your generation, you may not resonate with all of the perspectives presented here by your peers, but I do hope that the views of others will provide content for a healthy dialogue. As I listened to the experiences of young adults in ministry over the past several years, I found the insight, honesty, and passion of your generation inspiring. I also became convinced that this generation possesses a divinely instilled perspective to bring to God's work on earth in this season, whether in the local church, missions or community organizations, or other settings.

In order to fulfill this critical role, however, young ministers must recognize the responsibility to set aside personal preferences or ambitions that are inherent in our culture but inconsistent with God's purposes, and assume the work of carrying forth the work of God's kingdom! Furthermore, it is essential for Millennials to recognize the need for the perspectives and characteristics of other generations in ministry to fulfill God's purposes for this period of history. It may be tempting at times to simply assume an entrepreneurial spirit and start your own ministry initiatives. However, doing so without the support and wisdom of older generations will limit your effectiveness. There is much to be learned from their years of experience. While this book is directed primarily to those elder leaders, I believe there is much for you to gain as well. Thus, I have included notes to Millennials at the end of each chapter, and a chapter written specifically to you at the end of the book. Blessings as you pursue God's will!

PART I

Generational Traits

CHAPTER 1

Generations at a Glance

Why take the time to understand the implications of diverse generations in ministry today? The future of the church in North America demands we do so. One young youth pastor explained the situation we face: "I have seen so much devastation with young people in ministry. If they have a bad experience at a church, it almost ruins their call forever. I've seen it so often." Mainstream media, bloggers, and researchers have followed and commented extensively on the phenomenon of Millennials leaving the church. While this generational trend is important to understand, the loss of Millennials in church and ministry leadership is arguably the most pressing issue facing the church in America at this moment in history. Failure to pass the mantle of leadership effectively to the next generation threatens the kingdom work older leaders have dedicated their lives to fulfill. At this critical juncture, amid drastic social and cultural change, we are accountable to engage and effectively empower those who will carry the responsibility of serving, ministering, and leading in the uncertain days ahead.

Older leaders sometimes comment that young ministers must demonstrate more maturity or commitment before they can be entrusted with ministry opportunities, or be worthy of the time and effort required to mentor and develop them. While this might be ideal, it is unrealistic. Time is moving quickly. Most Millennials have graduated from college, and some are already taking senior leadership roles in ministry organizations and churches. Our window for engaging the calling they sense to ministry and empowering them for effective service is rapidly closing. One senior church leader confessed that three of the four Millennials who came to work at his church in the past few years have now left ministry altogether. It is unlikely they will ever return to full-time church work. This statistic is not uncommon. We cannot afford to hemorrhage young leaders at this rate.

So, how do we facilitate healthy intergenerational leadership within ministry contexts? The more mature leaders must assume responsibility to learn, adapt, and sacrifice in order to retain a generation for kingdom service. Adapting does not mean accommodating every need and desire we encounter in young leaders. It does, however, mean adjusting our expectations of where young staff members are now, in order to teach and develop them for future leadership challenges and roles. The consequences of not doing so are simply catastrophic for ministry leadership in the days to come. Furthermore, Millennials who truly feel a call to ministry must begin to contemplate the long-term consequences of their preferences and be willing to adjust their own expectations as needed. The balance of various generational perspectives allows for ultimate health within the body of Christ.

Multigenerational Leadership

Five generations coexist in the church today. Unprecedented diversity exists among the various age cohorts. Consider that the oldest of us witnessed World War II and the Golden Age of Radio. The youngest have never known a world without the Internet or without constant connection to people and events around the planet. The worldviews, perspectives, and desires represented across this expansive range of experiences are inevitably diverse. This incredible diversity elicits miscommunication and misunderstanding with devastating results, not only in the church, but in families, communities, and culture. Too often, the miscommunication and confusion that arise between young ministers and their leaders or churches and organizations result in Millennials choosing to leave formal ministry roles permanently. Efforts to facilitate healthy and realistic expectations and relationships must begin with understanding. Toward that end, let's look more closely at the generations in the church today.

The Silent generation was born between 1925 and 1945, during the Great Depression and World War II. They were raised by parents who enforced discipline, conformity, and obedience. As a result of the tumultuous times in which they were born, they value tradition, security, hard work, and respect. Silents understand the value of patience, delayed reward, and duty. Later generations owe much to the sacrifices they, their parents, and their grandparents made during a significant period in our country's history. To them, a career represented a means of living for which they were grateful, because they understood what it meant to go without. In their seventies and eighties now, most Silents are retired but they continue to influence denominations, churches, agencies, and organizations as founders, board members, and donors.

Baby Boomers were born between 1946 and 1964. Parental trends at the time focused on nurturing and pampering children. Coming of age during a period of relative prosperity and peace, Boomers entered adulthood with great optimism and drive. As the largest generation at the time, they forced culture, government, and industry to cater to their preferences and perspectives. As a result, Boomers often embody the narcissism and entitlement that are also seen in Millennials, a generation now surpassing the Boomers in numbers. For Boomers, work and career have been a central focus in life, and their hard work has contributed to the growth of many corporations, ministries, and churches. Boomers represent the senior leadership in most denominations and organizations today. In many cases, they represent the majority of decision-making positions. As they retire in the next decade or two, many churches and organizations will be scrambling to fill critical leadership roles for future growth and success.

Generation X was born between 1965 and 1979. As children, they experienced the explosive increase in divorce and daycare. Many paid the price for parental choices related to careers, ambitions, and relationships. As a result, they are often skeptical, independent, and pragmatic. Feeling hopeless, many checked out of society before they ever fully engaged. Generation X lives in the shadow of the larger generations preceding and following them. For many, career is a necessity that at times interferes with their lives. Nonetheless, they are realistic, balanced, competent with technology, and experienced in the workplace. Many Xers have learned to adapt and work effectively with Boomers as bosses and Millennials as colleagues. They offer much to the church as we face days of generational transition ahead.

Born between 1980 and 1995, today's young adults, also known as Millennials, constitute the largest generation in America's history to date. They are the most studied and observed generation on record. As they entered life, our society embraced the self-esteem movement, hoping a focus on building children's confidence would help negate a number of social issues. Parents put children first and supervised them closely. As a result, a generation of young people emerged that is protected, narcissistic, driven, and confident. At the same time, they are team players, willing to serve, and respectful of their parents and leaders. They differ in many ways from their older siblings and parents. (We examine more of these differences in the next two chapters.) Millennials view careers as a place to serve and find meaning. Retaining Millennials is proving to be a challenge for many corporations and organizations, including churches, missions agencies, and other parachurch organizations. This book responds to the dilemma of low retention and job satisfaction affecting many young adults in ministry today.

Generation Z, born after 1995, is still developing its cohort identity. So far, we know some significant factors affecting them and their emerging perspectives. Increasingly diverse, Generation Z will experience the end of the white majority in the U.S. during their lifetime. They are the first generation not only to experience complete exposure to technology since birth, but to have parents and other adults in their lives similarly engrossed by technology. They are posted, commented on, and liked via social media sites before they can even smile or talk. Other factors for Generation Z include declining economic opportunities, changing family structures, and an increasingly polarized political landscape. Time will tell how these and other factors will affect them long-term. In the meantime, the church must thoughtfully and prayerfully consider how we train and equip this developing generation.

The Call to Multigenerational Ministry

The context of church or ministry teams provides powerful opportunities for the diverse generations alive today to interact with and learn from one another as they serve God's kingdom. Second Timothy 3 gives us a powerful image of effective intergenerational mentoring and leadership in ministry. In verse 10, Paul tells Timothy, "You, however, know all about my teaching, my way of life, my purpose, faith, patience, love, endurance" (NIV). The apostle effectively shared the message and work he was called to with the next generation, modeling and mentoring Timothy for the work of the ministry. In verse 14, Paul challenges Timothy, "Continue in what you have learned and have become convinced of, because you know those from whom you learned it" (NIV). Paul could make this request of Timothy because he had made a significant investment into the life of this young leader.

In the next chapter, we begin to look at some of the specific ways in which Millennials differ from older generations in their views and practices regarding religion, church, and spirituality. These differences can be challenging to engage with and understand. As we delve into these topics, mature leaders reading this book will need wisdom and courage to apply Paul's model of intergenerational leadership to our context today.

To Millennial Readers

Have you ever grown tired of answering the technology-related questions of colleagues? Have you been embarrassed by comments that seem politically incorrect or antiquated? It is easy to focus on what someone who is older than you does not know or understand about the world you inhabit. However, have you ever stopped to ask people twenty or thirty years older than you what job skills they had to learn in their first job? Or what perspectives were popular when they were your age? My grandma regularly sends me text messages and "likes" my comments on Facebook. It takes a lot of effort for her to set up a new cell phone, and she often has questions for us grandkids about her computer. However, when I think of the skills she has learned over the course of her life, I am in awe of the knowledge, intelligence, and adaptability her life represents! As we talk about your generation in the next few chapters, make an intentional effort to find opportunities to understand the generations in whose footsteps you walk.

REFLECTION QUESTIONS

1. With which generational cohort do you most identify? Why?

2. Which generational cohort is most difficult for you to understand? How do the core values of your generation present obstacles in relating to team members from other generations?

3. Reflect on the intergenerational relationships in your life. Where are the most meaningful learning and mentoring opportunities occurring?

CHAPTER 2

Disengagement Epidemic

One of my young staff members sat slouched in the chair next to my desk. The expression on his face conveyed the frustration and defeat he felt. This was not a new conversation. He and I regularly discussed his perspectives and experiences serving formally and informally in the local church. As he left my office that day, I stared at the empty chair, recalling many similar conversations with other young adults over the years I had worked in Christian higher education. The conversations often echoed one another. Most involved dedicated young leaders, eager to serve. Then why the common and reoccurring thread of dissatisfaction and disengagement with churches and ministries where they volunteered, interned, and worked? What did they need in order to experience empowerment and encouragement for a future of participation in church and ministry leadership?

Millennials and the Church

A pastor recently asked me about recruiting Millennials to attend church membership classes. His thriving church boasts a large Millennial population in attendance. It possesses an authentic sense of community that draws young people, and numerous programs relate effectively to their needs. Nonetheless, church membership classes and business meetings attract primarily Silents, Baby Boomers, and a few Xers. Older church members, as a result, make most of the critical decisions for the congregation. Because they rarely become members, young people seldom participate on committees and leadership teams. Many churches and organizations across America experience this phenomenon of disengagement from formal processes and programs by young attendees or participants. Various factors contribute to this trend. Let's look at some of the most critical.

The Influence of Choice

Choice constitutes a powerful part of life for most young adults today. From childhood, Millennials experienced more options in life than any previous generation. Gone are the days when most parents told their children to eat what was put on their plates. Instead, we ask kids what they want to eat, what they want to watch, and where they want to go. Sam, a youth pastor, described his generation as the first to have entire channels that played cartoons all day long and department stores that offered every toy imaginable. The trend of choices continues into youth and adulthood. Coffee shops allow patrons to individualize their beverages in a dozen different ways, and smartphone apps permit users to set a variety of preferences to manage all the information users see and receive. Even educational programs, striving to meet the learning needs of each student, reinforced to this generation that they should always have what they need or what works best for them individually.

Too many choices and options may result in paralysis. Psychologists Amos Tversky and Eldar Shafir conducted insightful research on the dynamics of choice under conflict.[1] They found that the greater the number of available options, the greater the tendency to defer decision—sometimes indefinitely. Social psychologists Sheena Iyengar and Mark Lepper found that decisions made from a broad range of options, rather than a narrow range, resulted in lower satisfaction with the decision and haunting questions regarding the outcomes of the other potential choices.[2] For many young adults today, variations and alternatives surround significant life decisions such as education, finances, relationships, and religion. The options facing individuals often lead to decision paralysis. Millennials sometimes appear indecisive, noncommittal, and irresponsible because of the reality of many possibilities pulling at them. The sense that they may miss a better opportunity later by making an immediate or specific choice now often defers commitment to any choice.

Young adults expect consideration of individual preferences even when such consideration creates delay or results in indecision. More than older generations, Millennials deeply value and appreciate individuals as well as the needs, wants, and desires of individuals. This expectation impacts how they relate to the church and religion. Fewer and fewer young people buy in wholeheartedly to particular statements of faith or doctrinal beliefs put forth by denominations or church boards. They want the flexibility to choose the tenets of faith that resonate with their personal views and experiences. Prepackaged doctrinal statements do not allow for this level of preference. When it comes to their faith, Millennials shop around, looking for the best deal or product for their perspective or place in life. This mindset deters Millennials from joining membership classes or making a decision to adhere or commit to one particular congregation, denomination, or set of beliefs. It also allows them to avoid traditions or practices that lack biblical support or current relevance.

Religion or Spirituality

Millennials often equate established church organizations and doctrinal statements with formal religion and view them as impersonal, intolerant, and inflexible. After a year of serving on staff at a local church, Sean summed up the perspective of many young adults in America today: "Church to me is religion, a set of rules, a structure, and a tradition." Seemingly contradictory to their values, young adults often shy away from what they view as religion. For others, religion does not seem pertinent and therefore receives little consideration in their lives. Psychologist and professor Christian Smith, in his book *Souls in Transition,* identified many young adults as religiously indifferent or disconnected. These Millennials know or care little about religion in the first place or are simply alienated or disinterested in it altogether.[3]

A recent study by the Pew Research Center affirmed that Americans ages 18 to 29 are notably less religious than older Americans. One in four members of the Millennial generation is unaffiliated with any particular faith. Millennials are less likely to affiliate than Xers or their parents' and grandparents' generations were when they were young.[4] Despite these indicators of disengagement with formal religion and the established church, many Millennials do not view themselves as void of faith or spirituality. For those who do value a personal faith, many choose to identify themselves as "spiritual" rather than "religious."

While religion inherently brings with it prescribed belief systems, spirituality allows for greater openness and flexibility. It encompasses either mild interest in one's inner life or passionate commitment to a personal faith. Spirituality describes a wide variety of perspectives and faith traditions, and thus avoids disrupting relational harmony the way adhering to a specific religious code might. As I will discuss in more detail later, current culture effectively educates Millennials in the values of teamwork and tolerance. By choosing spirituality over a specific religious position, they distance themselves from the aspects of established religion that seem inconsiderate, discriminatory, disrespectful, or hateful. They sincerely pursue a sense of belonging and unity. Claiming a religious position that seems to alienate others lacks compatibility with current cultural values.

Strongly committed young adults who do adhere to a particular faith tradition or who practice a deep personal faith may still choose to avoid identifying with a particular religion. As popular culture continues to paint Christians as narrow-minded, inflexible, judgmental, or bigoted, young adults today inherently understand that aligning themselves with terminology or stereotypes that carry cultural baggage hinders their ability to relate to peers. Many still maintain an authentic commitment to personal faith, while avoiding traditional religious views or practices. Embracing a spiritual lifestyle, rather than a particular religion, does not require young adults to commit to any particular denomination or church. It allows them to honor cultural values, foster diverse relationships, and maintain a system of personal beliefs.

Church Attendance

Many local churches understand the challenges of engaging young adults in leadership roles and committed attendance. The Pew Research Center has indicated Millennials attend church services less often than older Americans do: only one-third of those under age 30 say they attend worship services at least once a week, compared with 41 percent of adults 30 and older and 50 percent of those over 65. As mentioned earlier, Millennials currently attend church or worship services at lower rates than Baby Boomers did at their age. Whereas 18 percent of Millennials currently report attending religious services weekly or nearly weekly, 26 percent of Boomers did so at their age.[5] The diminishing number of young adults faithfully attending church reflects the detachment occurring between Millennials and the church.

A Cross-Cultural Experience

The church's disengagement with the world Millennials inhabit today is a significant factor of young adult disengagement with the church. Challenges similar to those experienced in cross-cultural settings emerge as generational values collide in the church. When diverse values and practices collide, the results are often misunderstanding, frustration, and stereotyping. We typically believe our personal cultural approach is "right" and approaches that differ from ours are "wrong." When I teach cross-cultural communication, rarely do effectiveness, appreciation, and collaboration occur until individuals come to understand the worldview and cultural framework that informs unfamiliar behaviors they encounter. A task-oriented, time-conscious individual will tend to view an event-oriented, relationship-conscious business colleague who perpetually shows up late for meetings as irresponsible, disrespectful, and unreliable. The task-oriented individual must seek to understand the priority given to whatever event or conversation the colleague was engaged in before arriving at the meeting. Such an understanding will reveal that both have the same end in mind—building their company—but how they go about it often looks very different.

Comparably, the values, perspectives, and experiences of young adults today often differ sharply from those of older adults. Without mutual understanding, destructive perceptions often develop between groups. Older generations cannot hope to wait out the differences they see in the younger generations, mistakenly assuming young adults are simply passing through a "stage" they will outgrow someday. As I discuss in Chapter 4, the major cultural shift occurring today requires us to understand the language and perspectives of those who are in many cases choosing to leave the church altogether. A failure to do so will result in decreasing church involvement as Boomers continue to retire. Let's look at some of the areas where differences between the generations in the church often surface.

Vision and Purpose

I like to think of Millennials as a source of accountability to the church. Any group or organization, if left to function undisturbed, tends to drift toward apathy, the comfortable and familiar. The church often demonstrates this trend. We continue doing things one way because that is how we have always done them, or because that approach feels comfortable to those in leadership. Casey, a young man I interviewed, saw *new perspective* as an asset his generation brings to ministry: "We bring fresh eyes, a fresh view of where things stand and how things can be run." When Millennials encounter confusing practices or perspectives, they want to understand why things exist the way they do. Steeped in current trends of tolerance and open-mindedness, most young adults are willing to listen and seek to understand the opinions and ideas of others. This is where the church often forfeits valuable opportunities. Rather than embracing the "why" questions vocalized by Millennials as an opportunity to truly reflect on reasons for ministry practices being what they are, analyzing them in light of Scripture, and passing on valuable truths to the next generation, church leaders often view questions as a threat and effectively shut down any further discussion. This results in complete disengagement by the young adult truly seeking to understand the church, its vision, and its purpose.

Because young adults have so many options to choose from when it comes to church experiences and spiritual growth—a vast array of church sizes and varieties, books, online ministries, worship styles, and social media outlets—they want to clearly understand the vision and purpose of a church they are considering and what makes it unique. If they are going to choose one church or ministry over the many other options available to them, they need to feel confident in their decision. One young man I interviewed explained his experience as he sought to understand the vision of the church where he was working.

> I asked very specifically several times, "What is the vision of the church, what are we trying to accomplish?" The answer I got was a very vague, "We are here to reach the lost and disciple them," which should be the basis for every Christian church. So, there were no specifics, such as, "We're here to reach *this* type of lost people and we want to disciple them in *this* way." I assume there is more clarity to some, but when the executive pastor can't articulate that, I feel like there's a lack of understanding about what we are trying to do. I feel like sometimes the vision changed from one week to the next based on whatever the pastor wanted to do that week.

Another young leader had a very different experience. Carly explained her pastor's articulation of their church's vision to love people. She offered many specific examples of how she had experienced it and seen it practiced. In explaining how the vision permeated the church, she said, "A lot of people take their cue from Pastor Paul." Every program implemented at Carly's church originated with people and their needs and gifts. After several years in her position, Carly confirmed she could work for her pastor for many years to come. A clearly articulated and modeled vision had captured her commitment.

While the world of young adults today may seem foreign to older generations, experiences in the church often feel uncomfortable or confusing to Millennials. Taking the time to explain the meaning and purpose behind the functions and practices of the church can do much to bridge the generational divide. Churches desiring to attract and retain young adults need to be open to responding to questions regarding what the church believes and how it operates. A clearly articulated vision, lived out visibly, accomplishes much in winning the hearts of this generation and empowering them as they join more experienced leaders in ministry. We will discuss this component of vision further in chapter ten.

Authenticity versus Formality

While Millennials value a clear vision, they also need it communicated with authenticity. I recently taught a church leadership class comprised of lay leaders. Of the approximately two dozen people in the course, the majority were Baby Boomers. Out of curiosity, I asked what had led each of them to join their current church. The most common answer given was the quality of the formal teaching provided by the pastor. As I listened to the group discuss their perspectives in this regard, I could not help but reflect on how different the answers might be if the class had been comprised primarily of Millennials.

While the class participants I interacted with that day were highly satisfied by teaching that presented clearly articulated points, logical development of a topic, and appropriate scriptural support, many younger adults might find this presentation lacking in vitality. They can (and often do!) easily access thousands of similar teachings in seconds via the Internet. Furthermore, they have witnessed the hypocrisy of churches that preach one thing and often practice another. They are much more concerned with an authentic presentation, one that allows them to identify with the presenter and resonates with their personal lives as they seek to live out their church's vision and the Scriptures.

Nick, a young man struggling to understand the church, explained, "I just wanted Scripture to be real. I read Paul and it looked nothing like what we had, and I had no idea how to get there. . . . I was against preaching because all I heard was preaching, preaching, preaching, and I could see with my plain eyes things were not working." Nick echoes the frustration of many young adults who want Scripture to be real, who want to see it authentically taught and applied in the lives of those they choose to follow. The most impressive presentation possible will not compensate for authenticity in how we practice church and teach and live the gospel.

Meeting Needs

For young, passionate leaders entering the church to serve, the greatest cultural shock often occurs when the interests of people and programs clash. Just as they are not impressed by formal presentations devoid of authenticity, young adults are not impressed by extensive programs failing to meet real needs of people. When attuned to the culture of their peers, the chasm between where they see their friends and neighbors and where they see the church becomes overwhelming. One young church leader confessed, "I would just go into my office and cry because I felt like we weren't meeting the culture at all and I was just really passionate about it." He explained how he had graduated with a ministry degree and a heart and passion to minister to people. Once in his ministry position, however, he found his time consumed by planning the next great program. As time passed, his frustration grew because of the time and effort invested by the church in impressing young people with flashy programs and facilities. He asked, "Why don't we just save the wealth, save the effort, and put our time in where it's supposed to be—with the kids, mentoring them, and spending time with them?" He admitted, "I was looking at where we spend our time, and wondering if the programming was meeting the needs of the community." Other young church leaders I interviewed echoed a similar sentiment in regard to how churches manage their time and money in ministering to people. These questions arise from a passionate and sincere concern for people, one of the great gifts the Millennial generation brings to leadership roles.

Millennials have a heightened sense of the socioeconomic inequalities that exist in our nation today. Their values of teamwork and interconnectedness make it difficult for them to accept insensitivity, inequality, and any perceived inconsistencies in the financial stewardship of churches.

When I spoke to Gavin, the young leader expressed frustration with outreach programs at his church. Upon arriving in his new job on staff at a large church, his role evolved into helping with several of these programs. It quickly became apparent to him that the needs and challenges of individuals targeted by the programs were not being fully considered, but rather, programs emerged from what made the most sense for the church. He explained, "If you live in a trailer house that is 40 years old, and you are living paycheck to paycheck and trying to figure out if you are going to be able to pay your light bill this month, to go into this massive [church] building that is beautiful is probably going to make you feel uncomfortable." He went on to explain his frustration with the time and money being put into facilities and props for programming, while practical needs of people were being referred out to community organizations.

Similar patterns in spending led Jesse to resign from his position on staff at a church. His experience watching thousands of dollars being spent to update equipment that worked fine, but was not the latest technology, led him to question whether or not he could follow the vision of the church. He struggled to justify buying new couches for the church lobby or better projection systems for Sunday services rather than giving more to missions or local homeless shelters. He explained, "That really kind of started the process of feeling I couldn't support this vision. I think the pastor is a great man of God, I think the staff is incredible, but I can't stay."

These examples illustrate a few of the areas where Millennial perspectives conflict with current practices in the church and create a sense of culture shock for young adults seeking to engage in ministry. A lack of understanding of the biblical or historical basis for current ministry practices, disenchantment with formal presentations and programs, and seeming inconsistencies in effectively meeting the needs of people and communities all contribute to the disengagement epidemic we are experiencing. To better understand other areas of disconnect, it is important to understand the Millennial perspective and what sets them apart from other age cohorts. We turn to this in the next chapter.

To Millennial Readers

Unfortunately, to older generations, Millennials sometimes appear uncommitted and self-interested in the decisions (or lack thereof!) they make. When older leaders look at your life, do they see someone who is committed? Consider how your choices and actions reflect your level of commitment in relationships, work, church or community involvement, and education. How long do you typically stick with relationships, jobs, or volunteer opportunities? What are your typical reasons for leaving? Do those reasons demonstrate responsibility or personal interests and comfort? Self-motivation is evident in how you respond to difficult situations or projects. Do you give up easily, or do you problem-solve and persevere until you find a successful solution? Ministry leaders with years of experience have made significant sacrifices and endured seasons of hardship. They value investing in and mentoring young leaders who demonstrate the endurance and commitment to serve in long-term ministry. Strive to be someone worthy of their time and energy. How might you demonstrate your willingness to respect their legacy of leadership and to collaborate with them in leading present and future generations?

REFLECTION QUESTIONS

1. To what extent does your church/ministry/organization have a clearly understood and articulated vision? How is it communicated?

2. What venues does your church/ministry/organization provide for members to ask honest questions and receive specific feedback? Are young leaders encouraged and empowered to offer the valuable perspectives they bring to a ministry or team?

3. To what degree is your church/ministry/organization effectively understanding and meeting the needs of those you serve?

NOTES

1. Amos Tversky and Eldar Shafir, "Choice Under Conflict: The Dynamics of Deferred Decision," *Psychological Science* 3:6 (November 1992): 358–61.

2. Sheena S. Iyengar and Mark R. Lepper, "When Choice Is Demotivating: Can One Desire Too Much of a Good Thing?" *Journal of Personality and Social Psychology* 79:6 (December 2000): 995–1003.

3. Christian Smith, *Souls in Transition: The Religious and Spiritual Lives of Emerging Adults.* (New York: Oxford University Press, 2009), 295.

4. Paul Taylor and Scott Keeter, eds. "Millennials: A Portrait of Generation Next." Pew Research Center (February 2010): 85. http://pewresearch.org/millennials/

5. Ibid., 90–91.

CHAPTER 3

Divergent Worldviews

Kris, a youth pastor at a local church, identified both negative and positive characteristics of his generation as he reflected on his experience in ministry. "I think work ethic is maybe a lost art in our generation," he mused. He also noted the importance of passion and compatibility in empowering Millennials. "We struggle to find ourselves really pouring into something. I think once we can find our niche, we really invest in it, but if we don't find that, then we just kind of hang back and really don't invest."

Many leaders and managers of young adults have encountered these and other challenges as they have sought to engage the hearts and minds of Millennials in fulfilling the goals of a particular group or organization. The culture surrounding the early, formative years of today's young adults made a significant and lasting impact on their perspectives and worldviews. These often differ significantly from other generations and can create confusion or frustration. When we engage these differences, however, there is great potential to strengthen a team or organization. While there are always exceptions to any trend, the following discussion represents some general characteristics of Millennials that can give insight into the worldview of this generation.

Understanding Millennials

Millennials are the most studied generation in American history. Older generations respond with extremely mixed reviews to the unique characteristics and behaviors that the oldest Millennials bring with them into the workplace and leadership roles and that younger Millennials bring with them onto college campuses. It is important to remember the diverse groups reacting to Millennials. When Millennials first began to enter the workforce, four unique generational cohorts were already working side by side: the Silent generation, Baby Boomers, Generation X, and Millennials.

The oldest cohort, from the Silent generation, witnessed as children and young adults a world war and the incredible sacrifices made by many to ensure freedoms and opportunities often taken for granted by younger generations today. Baby Boomers, prior to Millennials, were the largest generation in American history, and remain very influential. Born amid great optimism, Boomers set out as young adults to right many of society's wrongs, propelling the Civil Rights Movement with its significant impact on our nation. Driven, career-focused, and disciplined, their solid work ethic contributed greatly to economic growth and progress as they took leadership roles. Generation X was born to busy, distracted parents who often prioritized other goals over them. They became the latchkey generation, at times independent, cynical, and closer to friends than family. The pendulum swung back again as Millennials entered the world and adults began to prioritize children and their needs. While intentions were positive, many believe this focused attention on young people produced mixed results.

Ironically, the characteristics individuals often find frustrating in other generational cohorts are in some cases of their own making. Children and youth do not raise themselves. Oftentimes, one generation unconsciously raises the next to complement, rather than reflect, their strengths and weaknesses. The seven core traits of the Millennial generation, as identified by social historians

Neil Howe and William Strauss, reveal the powerful effects of parenting and education on the emerging generation. These traits indicate that Millennials are special, sheltered, confident, team-oriented, conventional, pressured, and achieving.[1] Let's look at and other key characteristics in more depth.

Special and Confident

Born during the emergence of the self-esteem movement, Millennials have often heard they are special. Psychologists Nicole Lipkin and April Perrymore explained they are the first generation who got "Baby on Board" signs announcing their presence in moving cars. They are the first generation of "winners," because they were not allowed or able to lose in school and got gold stars or trophies just for showing up or participating in sports and other activities. They took cell phones to school, sent text messages instead of passing notes, and attended high school with metal detectors.[2]

While this recognition did produce increased confidence in many young people, the results of some of these factors have been negative, causing a sense of entitlement or narcissism. The technological world of social networking, in which they developed, reinforced a self-centered way of relating to the world. Young adults came of age tweeting, posting, and blogging about their lives for the world to read. Cultural experts Jean Twenge and W. Keith Campbell lamented, "Narcissism causes almost all of the things that Americans hoped high self-esteem would prevent, including aggression, materialism, lack of caring for others, and shallow values."[3] The messages meant to encourage Millennials throughout their childhood and youth instead reinforced in many a sense of entitlement that affects what they expect from churches, missions agencies, and other organizations they join.

One young missionary explained what agencies need to do to empower her generation. "If they want to get anything out of Millennials, they need to act like they care, even if they don't! We don't want to just be one in the crowd. We need to feel valued, and that people care about us." She went on to describe one supervisor she worked for who received her full support and energy. "He sowed into us and appreciated us; he validated us and he knew who we were as people. We would work extra for him even if we weren't getting paid. It wasn't even a question, because he cared for us. We need to know leaders have our back and they are proud of us." Julie, another young missionary, explained how her agency empowered her. "I don't feel like another number, another missionary. I feel like people know me and I'm important and valued." Millennials perform best when they feel special and appreciated!

Sheltered

This generation has also been sheltered. When I listen to my husband tell stories of childhood adventures with his two brothers, the stark differences between children's experiences then and now become readily apparent. While older generations spent much of their childhood playing outdoors, exploring and roaming their neighborhoods on foot or bike, building tree houses or forts, and imagining and role-playing for hours without parental presence, most Millennials lived their childhoods and youth within the protective confines of walls, fences, and gates. They experienced the monitoring of video cameras and GPS devices, the protection of bike helmets and safety belts, and the constant direction and guidance of their activities by adult supervisors. Unlike Xers, who at times experienced a lack of attention as latchkey kids, Millennials have been closely programmed, planned, enclosed, monitored, and directed by adults throughout their lives.

As young adults, Millennials often struggle to plan or organize their time effectively. Most went from school to sporting events, music lessons, tutoring, church activities, or other structured and adult-directed activities. Sam discussed the challenge: "Everything has been spoon-fed to the Millennial generation, and then we get into a job and we need to have practical mentoring and direction." He explained his tendency in his first ministry position to spend too much time on Facebook and Twitter because he did not know how to structure his time. He needed leaders to take the time to mentor and coach him. It was not until his second ministry role that he really received this support. When he did, however, it enabled him to become more effective in his position and calling.

The protection Millennials received as youth sheltered them from some life realities and contributed to their sense of confidence and trust in parents, leaders, and systems. Possibly more connected to their parents than any previous generation, Millennials often welcome parental involvement in their lives. This has held benefits for many young adults who find parents eager to help and support them. Entering young adulthood amid an economic recession, many have relied heavily on the support of parents to maintain their lifestyles in a difficult job market. For some, this means moving back home after college; for others, it means staying on Mom and Dad's cell phone plan and auto or health insurance, or receiving financial help for car maintenance or new clothes.

At times, the sheltered lifestyle of Millennials results in an inability to cope with failure or challenges effectively or maturely. Mom or Dad are often the first call a young adult makes in a moment of difficulty, relying on parental problem-solving or encouragement rather than handling the situation themselves. This may work in personal situations, but when expectations of parental support are projected onto teachers, leaders, and coworkers, it often results in frustration for everyone involved. (See Chapter 6 for more on this topic.) Involved parents sometimes impede the development of problem-solving capabilities and pose a threat to Millennial competence in areas of personal responsibility and independence. The sheltered lifestyle of this generation can increase the work required by churches, agencies, and organizations looking to empower them.

Lindsey explained her experience preparing for her first missions assignment. "I was coming fresh out of college; I had never lived in another country, so I was asking a lot of questions." Her sheltered and programmed lifestyle prior to entering ministry reflects the lifestyle of many of her peers. "Up to that point, I had been institutionalized, in school for 22 or 23 years, so for me to come out and not have very much structure was really difficult." She explained the need for organizations to understand this dynamic when working with young adults. "We are making our own choices for the first time in our lives, so a little structure would be nice."

Team-Oriented and Connected

While young adults bring challenges with them to the ministry environment, they also bring unique assets. Since childhood, they have learned the value of collaboration and team orientation. Not only do they feel connected to people around them, but through technology their sense of connection extends around the world. They possess an intuitive sense of shared experience and destiny with individuals who are very different from them, and they care deeply about the common good. A strong orientation toward social justice arises out of this sense of connectedness. Not only can they witness the needs of others via media, but social networking affords them a direct connection to the people who have the needs. In organizing short-term missions trips for many years, I have witnessed a dramatic shift from fifteen years ago when team members never communicated again with people they met around the world. U.S. students today often utilize e-mail, social networking sites, or text messages to stay in contact with those they meet while serving overseas.

The Millennial orientation toward teamwork produces a high tolerance for differences. The more rigid perspectives of older generations often appear judgmental, close-minded, or ignorant. Healthy intergenerational dialogue can help all parties learn from one another's worldviews and perspectives and minimize the frustration that otherwise occurs. As mentioned earlier, the sense of team and collaboration also lends itself to impatience with economic inequalities and a heightened sensitivity to how money is spent in light of known and existing needs.

Pressured and Achieving

Millennials often experience an intense drive and pressure to achieve. This results from parental and personal ambitions, increasing demands from technology and schools, and seemingly higher stakes as the job market and economy remain unpredictable. Furthermore, they feel the weight of living up to the expectation that they are special. Driven to achieve, they are arguably the busiest people in the U.S. Nonetheless, the effectiveness of Millennials in accomplishing what really matters is debated. While some applaud their creativity and innovative spirit, others denounce a seeming lack of commitment or endurance to see a project or initiative to completion.

Educator and author Tim Elmore has argued that Millennials really do desire to change the world; they just don't have what it takes to accomplish their lofty dreams. When the work becomes difficult or relationships become challenging, they change their minds and move on to something else. He identified a new term, "slacktivists," to represent this combination of achievement and non-commitment—Millennials are both slackers and activists.[4] In many cases, Elmore argued, young adults today have good intentions but lack the skills and ability required to navigate change in the complex world they inhabit.

Millennials possess the potential to achieve great things, but they could surrender to the complexity of their world or to disappointed expectations and thus jeopardize their dreams. They are a generation of contradictions. While mastering the world of technology, they expect quick and easy results; they are quick learners, but struggle with critical thinking and making commitments; they are competent at multitasking, but have difficulty focusing and persevering through difficult times; they want to be the best, but get easily discouraged when they fail; they desire to change the world, but anticipate doing it quickly and without sacrifice.

Professor and author Mark Bauerlein explained, "While teens and young adults have absorbed digital tools into their daily lives like no other age group . . . young Americans today are no more learned or skillful than their predecessors, no more knowledge-able, fluent, up-to-date, or inquisitive, except in the materials of youth culture."[5] The effects on relationships and long-term effectiveness for a generation that lacks patience, has deficient listening and conflict resolution skills, and is dependent on technology have yet to be determined. The potential impact of these realities for the future of American culture and society, as well as the organizations and institutions where young adults serve and lead, are significant.

Conventional

Millennials are often conventional in their approach to life. Howe and Strauss called them rule-followers and cited that from 1996 to 2006 rates of violent crime among Millennial teens fell by 70 percent, rates of teen pregnancy and abortion by 35 percent, and rates of alcohol and tobacco consumption hit all-time lows.[6] A recent study by the Berkley Center for Religion, Peace, and World Affairs identified the moral conscience of young adults, which often makes them appear more conventional than the Xers before them. However, the study revealed diversity in how Millennials decide what is right and wrong. Half of college-age Millennials embrace a universal approach to morality, believing in absolute rights and wrongs, while the other half take a more contextual approach, believing that situations dictate what is right or wrong.[7]

While Millennials appear more morally conscious than other generations at first glance, their struggles look different than we sometimes expect, and indeed, may be more complex than what we are used to seeing in the lives of young adults. Political and cultural writer Benjamin Brophy explained, "While levels of pre-marital and promiscuous sex are slightly falling among Millennials, they are instead indulging in Internet-packaged sex at a level unheard of for other generations."[8] Unfortunately, many Millennials justify some immoral behaviors because of a misinformed perception that they are not hurting anyone else. Their lack of critical thought and understanding of important issues often results in contradictory behaviors.

For example, Millennials advocate strongly for social justice. However, they widely participate in viewing pornography, the production of which usually occurs in connection with sex trafficking, one of the greatest social injustices of our day. So, while statistics do indicate Millennials have embraced a more conventional approach to life, their struggles are often more multifaceted and less tangible than those of other generations. This can make them extremely vulnerable and in need of mature role models.

Millennials demonstrate a value for tradition in their trust and respect for older generations. Many see the older generations as superior to the younger generation in several areas. They view their parents' generation as having a better work ethic, greater religious commitment, and being less entitled. This elicits respect from young adults and results in openness to hearing and receiving feedback and input from older adults who take the time to invest in their lives personally. While young adults are open to embracing many of the values of older generations, they also view themselves as more open-minded, educated, and tech-savvy. As a result, in some cases their generation's worldview trumps that of their parents on important issues. Ninety percent of Millennials agree their generation shares specific beliefs, attitudes, and experiences that set them apart from generations before them.[9] The years to come will reveal how the beliefs and characteristics delineated above will impact the future of this generation and our nation. In the meantime, the entrance of Millennials into the workforce is producing a powerful illustration of generational differences.

Generations Working Together

The workplace today boasts the greatest diversity among employees this country has ever known. Generational differences present varied perspectives that either enhance or disrupt team effectiveness and productivity. The collaborative nature of many employee groups today requires a concerted effort in managing these intergenerational teams. Understanding one another is essential, since tension in intergenerational relationships often emerges from behavioral expectations that conflict between peer groups. When gulfs of misunderstanding develop between the various age cohorts, communication and clarification regarding differences in values and worldviews become critical. In several key areas, the views of Millennials differ significantly from those of older generations.

Work/Life Balance

As previously suggested, Millennials enter the workforce with a different work ethic than did previous generations. In a traditional work ethic, embraced by most Silents and Baby Boomers, work comes first. For Millennials, personal life trumps work. Millennials have watched parents and other respected adults sacrifice personal goals and time with family and friends for the sake of companies, ministries, and the church, often without appreciation, recognition, or compensation. Coming of age in the midst of an economic recession, young people have observed many committed employees lose their jobs. Young adults today prefer to invest in what they know will last: their relationships and personal interests. This shift in priorities often appears irresponsible to older colleagues. However, Millennials approach work with a focus on taking care of themselves and protecting their priorities.

Growth and Advancement

Older generations often worked in one job for many years, using and developing a specific set of skills during that time. Today, young adults know their careers may consist of many jobs that require diverse skills as the workplace and world continue to change rapidly. A pioneer in the study of generations, Claire Raines explained that Millennials leave when a job does not meet their expectations, is repetitive or boring, or does not offer challenges and opportunities for development. They stay because of professional growth and personal satisfaction.[10]

Based on these insights, church leaders can accomplish much by asking about the passions and interests of young staff members. Finding ways to accommodate these interests amid other job responsibilities can greatly increase job satisfaction. If a job fails to respect their interests, to engage them in a meaningful manner, or to meet their expectations, Millennials are often quick to look for a new opportunity. When possible, organizations should allow for personal development. One young leader spoke appreciatively of serving at an accommodating church: "They gave me money for professional development, so I went to conferences; if I wanted to go on a personal retreat, I could go on a personal retreat." Even when funds are not available, providing flexibility in a young staff member's schedule to attend classes, seminars, or retreats is important. Professional development can even occur through book clubs, team discussions, and other informal and affordable venues.

Leadership and Authority

Perspectives on authority represent another area of difference between generations. With regard to authority figures, Millennials choose whom they follow. Leaders and bosses must earn respect, regardless of title and position. In contrast, other generations may endure or ignore authority figures, at times seeking or waiting to replace them. Nonetheless, they usually respect and defer to the role of the boss, something Millennials do not feel compelled to do. In fact, young adults tend to believe promotion and recognition should reflect accomplishment and effectiveness, and have little respect for seniority or experience as grounds for promotion if they believe the individual is incompetent. This dynamic creates tension between leaders and the young employees who do not respect them.

Technology and Communication

When it comes to technology, Elmore explained, Silents hope to outlive it, Boomers master it, Xers enjoy it, and Millennials employ it.[11] In my study of young adults in ministry, most found themselves in charge of media and online components of their churches and ministries simply because of their age, regardless of whether these tasks were in their job description. This generational expectation created frustration for many young adults. While Millennials effectively use technology, they often resented the expectation to manage it for the organization and constantly help others with related problems or projects.

Technology changes how young adults approach their jobs. Because it often enables them to work twenty-four hours a day, the regular eight-hour work day can seem confining or impractical. They desire to use technology while working to stay connected to important relationships. For many young adults, technology enables efficiency and leads to a belief that work should be measured by what is accomplished, rather than how long it takes. Sometimes technology proves distracting to the work that needs attention. Technology use deemed inappropriate by a leader or organization needs to be clearly communicated to young employees from the start to avoid future frustrations.

Communication is an important component of successful intergenerational teams. Effective communication includes over-communication, anticipates generational needs, and empowers individuals to contribute their strengths to a team. The efficiency of technology creates an expectation in young adults of quick responses to communication. E-mails, text messages, or other communications they send should be acknowledged promptly and responded to in a timely manner. Some older employees may find the communication of young colleagues frustrating as it can seem brief, sloppy, or tactless. Common communication guidelines and expectations, along with training in areas needing attention, can improve team interactions and alleviate frustrations. The importance of effective communication on the part of leaders working with young adults will be discussed further in chapter ten.

Compensation and Benefits

In most cases, young adults enter jobs anticipating they will be short-term, although the right leadership and motivation can result in Millennials committing for many years to a company or ministry. While higher pay is often an enticement for older workers to transfer jobs, many young adults find that meaningful employment, good leadership, effective teams, and a good environment for their family can possess as much appeal as money. They do value, however, feeling fairly compensated through wages and benefits. Malachi appreciated the first church he worked at as a youth pastor. "They did a nice job; they paid me fairly. I wasn't underpaid; I wasn't overpaid." He also noted other benefits in that job, such as support, a flexible schedule, and professional development opportunities. He remained in the role for four years, which is longer than most young adults anticipate staying in a position.

Casey, a youth and family pastor, talked about his struggle regarding compensation in ministry roles. In college, his ministry professors told him there was not a lot of money in his chosen profession. He described the influence of a meaningful experience ministering to young people one summer during college. "I was considering switching to a business administration major, but that really solidified it for me. This is what I want to do; it is not about the money. . . . That is what I am still telling myself: it is not about the money!" Employers who can give fair wages and benefits such as meaningful work experiences, support for the interests and passions of the young leader, healthy leadership and teams, flexibility in work schedules, and opportunities for personal development will increase the likelihood of retaining competent young leaders.

While intergenerational differences often produce challenges within the workplace, they also reflect the changes present in society. In the following chapter, we will look at some significant cultural shifts occurring around us. They indicate that the diverse perspectives present in the workforce today are more significant than simply a generation gap.

To Millennial Readers

Do you work with leaders you find difficult to understand? How do you think they perceive you? Have you asked them? Take the initiative to foster a relationship with them! Listen when they talk and watch their actions. Observe what they value and why. Take the time to ask for advice in their areas of expertise. Follow their advice when applicable, and demonstrate that you value what they bring to the team or organization. Inquire about what led them to pursue ministry and thank them for years of faithful service! Even if you still find a leader difficult to follow, you may learn some valuable lessons as you listen and watch.

REFLECTION QUESTIONS

1. What are the most significant generational differences in your team/workplace? Does everyone feel they have a voice, or do people favor some perspectives over others? How can all team members better foster understanding and unity?

2. To what extent do employees in your church/ministry/organization feel satisfied with the level of benefits and opportunities provided? What additional benefits and opportunities could the organization offer that would be appreciated by diverse team members?

NOTES

1. Neil Howe and William Strauss, *Millennials Go to College: Strategies for a New Generation on Campus (2nd Edition)* (Great Falls, VA: Lifecourse Associates, 2007), 59–60.

2. Nicole A. Lipkin and April J. Perrymore, *Y in the Workplace: Managing the "Me First" Generation* (Franklin Lakes, NJ: Career Press, 2009), 15.

3. Jean M. Twenge and W. Keith Campbell, *The Narcissism Epidemic: Living in the Age of Entitlement* (New York: Free Press, 2009), 9.

4. Tim Elmore, *Generation iY: Our Last Chance to Save Their Future* (Atlanta: Poet Gardner Publishing, 2010), 27.

5. Mark Bauerlein, *The Dumbest Generation: How the Digital Age Stupefies Young Americans and Jeopardizes Our Future [Or, Don't Trust Anyone Under 30]* (New York: Penguin, 2009), 8–9.

6. Howe and Strauss, 15–16.

7. Robert P. Jones, Daniel Cox, and Thomas Banchoff, "A Generation in Transition: Religion, Values, and Politics among College-Age Millennials," Public Religion Research Institute, Inc. and Georgetown University's Berkley Center

for Religion, Peace, and World Affairs (2012), 24, accessed August 17, 2013, http://repository.berkleycenter.georgetown.edu/120419BC-PRRIMillennial ValuesSurveyReport.pdf.

8. Benjamin Brophy, "My Generation's Disease," *The American Spectator* (May 17, 2013), accessed April 17, 2014, http://spectator.org/articles/55571/my-generations-disease.

9. Eric Greenberg, *Generation WE: How Millennial Youth Are Taking Over America and Changing Our World Forever* (Emeryville, CA: Pachatusan, 2008), 14.

10. Claire Raines, *Connecting Generations: The Sourcebook for a New Workplace* (Berkeley: Axzo Press, 2003), 122.

11. Elmore, 24.

CHAPTER 4

More Than a Generation Gap

"You've got to be willing to change!" Nick declared emphatically as we discussed the church in the United States today. He explained that, for most Millennials, everything in their lives has changed frequently. His understanding of change revealed the perspective of the emerging generation.

> I have this theory that no other people in the history of humanity have had to change like we're going to have to change. We are going to have to able to accept change repeatedly every decade. Just think about ten years ago, how much has changed since then? I'm going to get to age 50 and I'm going to have to change; I'm going to get to age 60 and I'm going to have to change. If the church can be committed to the vision and not how it gets done, so the pastor can provide the vision and hold loosely to how it is accomplished, that's key.

The rapid changes occurring in our society today are both broad and deep. They range from significant cultural shifts to minute details in our everyday lives. Rapidly emerging perspectives colliding with traditionally established norms represent more than a generation gap.

Generational Theories

One of the frequent questions I receive when discussing Millennials is whether the characteristics they exhibit are simply a result of their stage in life. It is true each generation depicts some similar behaviors and perspectives at particular stages of their life cycle. This is sometimes referred to as maturational theory, the understanding that developmental stages or norms inform typical observable behaviors or beliefs as people age. For example, many teenagers go through periods of desiring and exercising independence. Young adults tend to be more idealistic than their parents or grandparents who have more life experience. However, there are also unique aspects to each generational cohort.

A generational cohort typically spans a basic phase of life, roughly twenty years. Three primary factors or theories explain the formation of a generational cohort. These include *life cycle effects* or maturational theory, those characteristics more prominent at specific developmental stages; *period effects*, which are major events experienced simultaneously by all members of the cohort at a certain stage in development, also called generational theory; and *cohort effects* or life-course theory, describing how major events impact the lifelong perspectives of a group.

Historians and sociologists Neil Howe and William Strauss reiterated what makes the cohort-group truly unique is that all its members encounter the same national events, moods, and trends at similar ages. Since history affects people very differently according to their age, common age is what gives each cohort-group a distinct biography.[1] Shared experiences at specific life stages result in common sense-making and group norms that can be confusing to other age cohorts. The personality and perspectives of Millennials, the largest generation in American history, are now beginning to show their impact on society as the oldest are in their early thirties and the youngest enter college.

In their groundbreaking 1991 book *Generations*, Howe and Strauss developed a theory on generational cycles that claims a repeating pattern in how cohorts respond to each other and the world around them. The repeating pattern of generations illustrates ebbs and flows in culture and perspectives. They also identified two types of social moments with power to propel generational cycles. The first is a *secular crisis*, with an outward focus on society reordering its institutions and behavior. The second is a *spiritual awakening*, focused more on the inner world of values and beliefs.

Howe and Strauss asserted these social moments are predictable and regular.[2] Their analysis proposed the next secular crisis would occur as Millennials entered adulthood.[3] Interestingly enough, the terrorist attacks of September 11, 2001, occurred as the oldest Millennials were in college, and seven years later a worldwide economic recession drastically affected the environment in which young adults seek to establish their adult lives. Howe and Strauss indicated a secular crisis and the response could result in the nation's public life undergoing significant transformation.[4]

While many view generational differences today as simply that—differences—a deeper look reveals that we are in fact in the midst of a significant societal and cultural shift, one that could reshape fundamental understandings of the world for years to come. Millennials stand on the edge of this transformation, a chasm dividing the past from the future. For those called to ministry, their task will be to successfully lead churches and organizations through the future consequences of current trends. While the older generations strive to preserve what has worked in the past, the emerging generation will be entrusted with identifying strategies for the viability and growth of churches and ministries in the future. They need equipping to do so effectively amid a culture in transition.

Environment of Change

The 2010 U.S. Census confirmed Nick's sense of significant change. Indeed, changes that have occurred over the past twenty years have left sociologists and demographers stunned. While many of the shifts occurring in our country were anticipated, the rate at which they have occurred is unprecedented. Today, our nation is much larger, older, more nontraditional in regard to marriage and family, and more Hispanic and Asian than it was in 1990. It would also appear the fascination with children that occurred as Millennials entered the world is shifting to some extent, as many young adults are less enamored with having children or are waiting until later in life to start families. Much of America's social and cultural makeup is being redefined, and the impact could influence everything from elections to social expectations for years to come.

Many developments in the past two or three decades have changed how we live our everyday lives and further represent the rapid change we must navigate in our society today. When most Millennials were infants or young children, Amazon.com did not exist. For that matter, there was no such thing as online shopping, online gift registries, eBay, Netflix, or Google. One could not type a question into a browser and instantly receive endless answers and opinions from individuals around the globe. It was not until 1991 that the World Wide Web was launched. Today, most of us cannot imagine life without it. The scope of change we have experienced since then with social networking and globalization brings into perspective the magnitude of change we could experience in the next two to three decades.

Their place in history provides Millennials with the agility and understanding that can help churches pioneer innovative ministry methods in a changing world. One of the greatest struggles for Casey and his peers in ministry is the realization that they have very little ability to effect change in ministries where they serve. "Coming out of college you have all these great ideas; they are paradigm-shifting [ideas]. Churches are dying; congregations are not relevant to our culture. You have ideas about how you are going to change things, and then you come into it and realize you will be lucky if you get even one of those ideas through in your first two years." For Millennials, who grew up conditioned to experience instant gratification, this adjustment is difficult. Casey explained an important realization he had made: "Everything you want to do takes time; not to say that it won't happen, but it takes time and patience." For churches and ministries, however, the question emerges, "How long we can afford to wait to make critical changes to position us for future success?"

The thought of swift and continuous change can be disorienting, yet adaptability is an essential element of growth and effectiveness in ministry. Too often, methods are believed to be as sacred as the truth they have been used to convey. The challenge entails holding firmly to the truth of Scripture while adjusting methods as our environment changes. One youth pastor expressed the perspective of many young ministers: "I feel the church in general has always been a step behind; we're always playing catch-up with what's happening in culture or society." While making significant changes feels overwhelming, this season is not the first time the church universal has faced the challenge. A look at historical context provides some much-needed perspective.

Historical Context

Western history reveals significant shifts in culture every few hundred years. Management consultant and educator Peter Drucker indicated we are currently living through such a transformation, and within a few decades society will rearrange itself as well as its values, social and political structures, and key institutions.[5]

Many others agree with the assessment that we are in the midst of a significant change in Western, even global, society. Pastor and author Chuck Smith Jr. called it a "cultural fault line between two epochal periods."[6] The transition between the modern era and the postmodern era is perceived by some to be as significant as the shift that propelled the world out of the Middle Ages five hundred years ago.[7] A more recent cultural shift in Western society occurred around the time of the American Revolution and resulted in such ideologies and movements as capitalism, communism, and the Industrial Revolution—all of them powerful influences of the modern era.

The modern era in the Western world centered on the Enlightenment, a project of the mid-eighteenth century. "The idea [of the Enlightenment] was to use the accumulation of knowledge generated by many individuals working freely and creatively for the pursuit of human emancipation and the enrichment of daily life."[8] The promise of scientific domination of nature included freedom from scarcity and want. Modernism held to a universal worldview and moral standard, a belief in knowledge as good and certain, and truth as absolute. Individualism was valued while thinking, learning, and beliefs were determined logically. Postmodernism and relativism challenged many of these ideas and characteristics. Young people today, disillusioned by the broken promises of modernism, are willing to accept new and different ways of thinking and interacting with the world. Their exposure to the world and experience of it are far more multicultural and global than in past generations—and their disappointment with current circumstances inspires them to broaden their horizons to accept wisdom from anywhere and everywhere. They are ready to accept change.

Social theorist David Harvey explained that, somewhere around 1970, we see postmodernism emerge as a full-blown, though still incoherent, movement out of the roots of the anti-modern sentiments of the 1960s.[9] Postmodern philosophers applied theories of deconstruction to the world as a whole, attacking the modernist concepts of universal meaning or a supreme center to reality. The widely accepted beliefs in a timeless, absolute truth or in salvation by society, as promoted by Marx, began collapsing under postmodern thought. A significant change emerging from postmodernism is the valuing of all truth as valid, especially as determined in the contexts of specific communities.

Drucker indicated this period we are now experiencing is but a transition, and will not be permanent. "What will emerge next, we cannot know: we can only hope and pray. Perhaps nothing beyond stoic resignation? Perhaps a rebirth of traditional religion, addressing itself to the needs and challenges of the person in the knowledge society?"[10] Christian theologian and ethicist Stanley Grenz acknowledged that postmodernism poses potential dangers. Nonetheless, he argued, "It would be ironic—indeed, it would be tragic—if evangelicals ended up as the last defenders of the now-dying modernity. To reach people in the new postmodern context, we must set ourselves to the task of deciphering the implications of postmodernism for the gospel."[11]

Traits of Modernism and Postmodernism Affecting the American Church

Modernism	Postmodernism
Confidence in reason to discover truth	Acceptance of self-determined, pluralistic views
Power and faith in human reasoning	Power and faith in personal experience
Communication driven by the printing press	Communication driven by Internet and media
Mechanical, structured	Organic, open
Creation	Deconstruction
Individualism	Community
Objectivity	Subjectivity
Distance	Participation

The current state of flux in cultural values and perspectives provides the backdrop for Millennials coming of age in our society. Christian theologian and philosopher Francis Schaeffer explained, "Most people catch their presuppositions from their family and surrounding society the way a child catches measles."[12] In the current postmodern society, many families, teachers, and leaders are encouraging young people to make their own decisions about values and religion and to be tolerant of all beliefs. These decisions influence not only the direction of culture, but also individual lives and actions. According to Schaeffer, the flow of history and culture is rooted in the thoughts of people. The inner life of the mind, with its perspectives and worldview, determines our actions and value systems.

Young people today have experienced the effects of a society in transition and evolving values their entire lives. Their mental, physical, social, and spiritual development has occurred in a culture wrestling to release itself from the influences of modernism with its structures, hierarchy, and dependence on reason. Their education and formation are rooted in the influences of relativistic and deconstructionist views. As a result, the perspectives and behaviors of emerging young adults often look drastically different than those of their parents or grandparents. Dan Kimball, a leading voice in the early Emergent Church movement, explained, "What we are experiencing in our culture is not merely a generation gap but a change in how people view the world."[13] As young adults step into leadership roles in ministry, the factors that have influenced their understanding of the world will impact their engagement in the church as we move further into the twenty-first century and whatever lies beyond.

To Millennial Readers

As mentioned earlier, your generation has been told you are special from a young age. I believe that message is prophetic of the role you must fill through this tumultuous period of history. It is a special role, a God-given role. Ironically, your generation has been deceived by an inaccurate depiction of what that "specialness" actually means. Rather than attention, entitlement, and comfort, it likely means humility, sacrifice, and, for some, suffering. Your challenge now becomes embracing a new definition of being a "special generation." My husband served in the military for many years. Important missions for him rarely meant a pleasant or enjoyable experience. Rather, they represented difficulty, danger, and discomfort, but ultimately fulfillment and joy in knowing the work accomplished meant freedom and safety for others. The mission of the Millennial generation is not so different in nature. It means navigating unknown territory as society changes, encountering cultural forces bent on undermining truth, standing firm for God and God's purposes, and devotedly passing faith on to future generations. May you be strengthened and inspired to be the "special" generation you are called to be for the sake of God's kingdom in this season of history. You have the prayers and support of many of us who have gone before you (Hebrews 12:1-3).

REFLECTION QUESTIONS

1. What is your response to the claim that our culture is significantly changing? Why?

2. What challenges do modern or postmodern ideas and trends present your church/ministry/organization?

3. How should your church/ministry/organization take active steps to respond to cultural shifts that are occurring?

NOTES

1. Neil Howe and William Strauss, *Generations: The History of America's Future, 1584–2069* (New York: William Morrow and Company, 1991), 48.

2. Neil Howe and William Strauss, *The Fourth Turning: An American Prophecy* (New York: Broadway Books, 1997), 40–41.

3. Ibid., 51.

4. Howe and Strauss, *Generations*, 15.

5. Peter Drucker, *Post-Capitalist Society* (New York: HarperCollins Publishers, 1993), 1.

6. Chuck Smith Jr., *The End of the World as We Know It: Clear Direction for Bold and Innovative Ministry in a Postmodern World* (Colorado Springs: WaterBrook Press, 2001), 12.

7. Drucker, 2–4.

8. David Harvey, *The Condition of Postmodernity: An Enquiry into the Origins of Cultural Change* (Cambridge, MA: Blackwell Publishers, 1990), 12.

9. Ibid., 3.

10. Drucker, 13.

11. Stanley J. Grenz, *A Primer on Postmodernism* (Grand Rapids: William B. Eerdmans Publishing Company, 1996), 10.

12. Francis A. Schaeffer, *How Should We Then Live? The Rise and Decline of Western Thought and Culture* (Old Tappan, NJ: Fleming H. Revell Company, 1976), 20.

13. Dan Kimball, *The Emerging Church: Vintage Christianity for New Generations* (Grand Rapids: Zondervan, 2003), 59.

PART II
Millennial Values in Ministry

CHAPTER 5

Business as Usual

Emily, an administrative assistant at her local church, coordinates many details related to logistics, programming, and communication. A Millennial, she works primarily with Baby Boomers. I recently sat down with the staff at her church to talk about intergenerational dynamics and how they affect leadership teams and overall ministry effectiveness. As we discussed current trends in church practices and the values of young leaders, she nodded emphatically. The importance of family and relationships for her generation emerged from the conversation, and she exclaimed to the group, "This is why I insist on calling it a congregational meeting, *not* a business meeting!" We had hit on a critical factor for many young adults entering ministry. Rather than the community they expected when they chose to pursue ministry as a career, many encounter the church as a business. This discovery can be both disappointing and disenfranchising.

Running It Like a Business

Sometimes the business culture in churches and ministries today is subtle, other times it is overt, yet it seldom goes unrecognized by young leaders. When I talked with Gavin, he described a long-time staff member at his church who said, "We're going to run it like a business." Gavin acknowledged that to "a certain extent you do have to run it like a business because if you don't have money to pay the rent, you don't have a church. So there was definitely a business side to the church." He described his leaders defining success as whatever would keep the doors open. That approach served to disenfranchise this young staff member.

Entering the workforce during an economic recession, Millennials are well aware of the financial challenges facing local churches. Many experienced significant staff and budget cuts while serving in their first ministry positions. One young man explained that the main priority of the church where he served was the weekend service. "It was even described in that way, that during this tough time (economic recession), we're just going to focus on the weekend service. We have to cut something, so things are going to get cut outside of the weekend service." While acknowledging the excellence of the weekend programming, the young leader found the focus somewhat disconcerting: "It was not a problem to spend several thousand dollars on a weekend service for a prop they were going to use one time." Ongoing spending on programming and facilities amid deep staff cuts at the church communicated a value on programming over people. How a church decides to allocate resources communicates to young leaders the priorities of the church.

In my study on the generational values of Millennials in regard to the church and ministry, a definite shift from many current ministry practices emerged. In the next two chapters, we will examine the Millennial view of ministry. In many instances, a vision of the church as a family clashes with existing practices of the church as a business. For young adults I met, working at an organization that embraced their values proved important to job satisfaction and retention. As a new generation steps into leadership in many U.S. churches, some adjustments may be in order.

How We Got Here

As Millennials enter leadership in church cultures defined largely by Boomer values, it is important to remember what factors are at play. Pastor and author Dan Kimball has observed that Christianity was born as a faith or religion, and as it moved through history, it took on characteristics of a philosophy in Greece, a legal system in Rome, and a culture in Europe. Arriving in America, Christianity took on many characteristics of big business.[1] Boomer values of social progress, careerism, and upward mobility have often reinforced this business model of conducting church.

Over the past few decades, titles and positions within hierarchical church structures have changed to resemble those found in the business world. Terms such as *executive, associate,* and *assistant* in pastoral and ministry titles more closely reflect what young adults see in the corporate workplace than what they understand of biblical models of leadership. As titles in the religion sections of local bookstores began to reflect the titles and concepts in the business management sections, church leaders began applying business principles, language, and metaphors to many aspects of the church.

Staff meetings started to include agenda items such as marketing, branding, or strategic planning. Leadership teams sought to pursue excellence, relevance, and effectiveness. How they measured these elements was often in the condition or size of buildings, the money in offering plates, or the number of converts and bodies in the pews on Sunday morning. Millennials are intuitively sensitive to these measurements when applied to spiritual growth and success, and many respond negatively to the practice of ministry as business.

Responding to Ministry as Business

Young leaders do not deny the value of some corporate or business practices in the local church or in ministry organizations. However, they do respond strongly to those practices taking precedence over the needs or interests of people. In many instances, the younger generation is responding not simply to what may be important business elements, but rather to the valuing of the corporation of the church over its people. Peter Haas, author and pastor to growing numbers of unchurched twenty-somethings, termed this idea "corporate subservience." He defined the principle of corporate subservience as "the moment the corporation becomes equal to (or greater than) the spiritual body in terms of focus, or energy."[2] The corporation of the church, such as programs or buildings, should serve the spiritual body or people of the church. Haas claimed that the moment people become essential in maintaining the corporation of the church and decisions reflect what is best for the corporation, the church has become subservient to the corporate aspects of its functioning.

Money

Perhaps most central to the Millennial experience of corporate subservience in church and ministry is the management of money. They understand the need and value of money and resources, but are likely to regard finances in ministry much differently than older generations do. Young leaders want the people and purpose of the ministry to take precedence over the financial demands that arise or exist. When leaders make unwise financial decisions, the pressure of making payments or sustaining overhead costs can overshadow the real purposes of an organization.

Kate explained that the church where she served as a staff member "was all money-oriented." She described working in the church office after services and wanting to discuss the sermon or people with the pastor. His first question to her was always the same: "What was the offering?" She felt as though the pastor was in denial about the reality of the church's priorities and effectiveness. "The truth was, we couldn't pay the gas bill, we couldn't pay the electric bill, and we couldn't pay our mortgage," she recounted, and in her experience those concerns took precedence over the well-being of the people.

Many young adults possess an aversion to the connection of money with ministry. In cases where fundraising was required, those I interviewed often expressed a discomfort in asking for money. Levi reported starting a new ministry. "Financially-speaking, there was no budget, so I had to raise a budget. I am an awful fundraiser. I hate asking people for money." As a result, he ran the ministry without a budget. Sam expressed similar hesitations. "I hate fundraisers. I don't want to do a fundraiser and ask people for money for youth ministry." While they appreciated the need for money, they were hesitant to request funds for their ministry efforts.

For young adults feeling called to serve overseas or in volunteer ministry positions, raising a full-time salary can seem overwhelming. Methods prescribed by many organizations feel awkward and uncomfortable because the approaches do not reflect Millennial values. Lindsey, a young missionary who has served overseas for two years, explained how she appreciated the fundraising training she received from her organization, but in retrospect, something was lacking. She felt pressured to follow the program her leaders laid out, which focused on getting money, not necessarily building relationships.

"I think there is something very personal about your relationship with supporters and it is not just about money," Lindsey observed. "And if it is just about asking as many people as possible, to me that's begging, because I'm asking you for money but not valuing your friendship. Relationships take time, and personal communication takes time." After a couple of years in ministry, she recognized the value of young leaders being encouraged to find what works for them and realized that, in the end, it is not just about money, but about finding supportive people.

Ana, another young missionary, explained, "I don't think anyone really trains you how to fundraise, or build relationships with pastors or missions committees, or just friends and people you meet. They have to be people to you; they can't just be dollar signs." Millennials do not just want money; they want people to care. This perspective arises out of the Millennial value of relationships and family over business in ministry settings (see Chapter 6 for more on this).

Financial practices deemed necessary or appropriate by some in ministry often fail to reflect the most important ministry goals of young adults. For them, relationships take priority over money. Many young leaders desire simpler, more intimate forms of ministry that require less money. Jesse described how he wanted to run events for his youth ministry through the small groups at his church, thus eliminating a lot of pressure on leaders to come up with large events and minimizing ministry costs. He felt students valued having a spaghetti dinner and watching a movie together at a leader's house. When he requested permission to make this shift in his ministry, his leader denied the request, and Jesse was required to plan an expensive, large-scale event instead.

Nick also discussed feeling a discrepancy between how his church spent money and what he really valued in ministry. When his church spent $15,000 on new stage lights, Nick began to question if the church's priorities were correct. He expressed a desire to simply work with people, and not worry about impressing them with a show. To him, that involved having them over to his house, taking them on retreats, and spending time with them. Those aspects of ministry did not require a lot of money.

When explained effectively, young leaders understand the purpose behind strategic spending, even when they do not agree with it. One young pastor described how everything his church did was to bring people to Christ. Even expensive technology purchases targeted business people who wanted to be at a church that emphasized excellence, because in their businesses they were accustomed to excellence. In describing the methods employed at his church, the young pastor explained they did everything they could "to bait or to excite people, not for the sake of excitement, but to get them in so God can speak to them and work in their lives." He acknowledged every church should embrace that philosophy to some degree.

Because many Millennials benefit from the financial investments and comforts other generations provide, time must reveal if their perspectives will change when the decisions and responsibility rest on *them* to pay for the lights and air conditioning, provide safe and fun facilities for childcare, and purchase technology to simplify ministry tasks.

Numbers

For Millennials, money is not the only disappointing standard of success in regard to ministry effectiveness. For many, the number of people in a church is not nearly as important as what is happening in the lives of those people. Gavin explained his perspective: "When we did the Wednesday night classes, success was measured by how many people showed up to the event." His frustration arose out of a differing view of success. He believed the true measure of success should entail transforming people's lives, creating relationships and a support network, and empowering everyone in the church to reach and encourage even more people. He emphasized equipping those who did attend an event to go out and encourage others so that ministry would not be confined within the church walls.

Levi described the counting of attendees at his church. At weekly staff meetings, the whole staff would go through a member roster to count exactly how many people had attended the past weekend. He explained the intention of this was "to make sure our numbers were good, make sure our numbers were right." Even though someone counted on Sundays, they reviewed the list "to bolster the numbers we had counted. If someone was in the children's ministry or someone was going to the bathroom, this would make sure our numbers were as good as possible." He did not know of any purpose for collecting this information, such as pastoral care follow-up, other than the pastors and board wanting to know the numbers.

Jacob described the intense pressure his senior pastor felt to bring in more people so he could have a paycheck. He explained, "We were literally making graphs of our attendance every week, and he made me make a graph of the youth." While understanding the tension his pastor felt, Jacob argued, "You have to fight against that and say, 'We are going to preach the gospel no matter what.' I think the biggest struggle we face is when we treat church like a business, rather than a place to proclaim God's glory."

Carly's experience illustrated different priorities, more compatible with Millennial values. At her church, much like Levi's, every Monday the staff would sit down and review the church roster. In this case, the purpose and intention for collecting this information was clear. She explained how they marked off every single person they saw the previous Sunday because they valued relationships and made an effort to connect with as many people as possible each week. When they identified people who had not been at church, they sent the bulletin to them, and if individuals missed two weeks, they received a personal call from a staff member. Carly related some of the valuable interactions and discoveries about people's lives that these phone calls produced. While the process of noting those in attendance resembled what occurred in Levi's church, the focus on relationships rather than numbers was energizing, rather than distressing, to the young leader.

Malachi's perspective illustrated the emphasis many Millennials place on growth and transformation in the lives of individuals over the urgency of large numbers. He described his personal philosophy of ministry as "thinking more about developing a Jesus-like ministry, [with] two, three, or four [people] that you are investing in intimately, and maybe a greater twelve you are in close relationship with, but you invest with a few." He explained that this perspective kept him from becoming frantic about numbers. "I will invest in these three, and if three more show up, great; if thirty show up, great, if three hundred show up, great. I can only invest in these three, so it takes a little pressure off trying to develop a big ministry, because if it is big, I am going to teach the Bible; if it's small, I am going to teach the Bible."

Ana described a similar ministry philosophy. "Loving God and people is the most important thing. If I am all about numbers and I have one hundred people who don't feel loved by me, they probably are not going to feel loved by God either. If I have two people who feel loved by me, they are probably going to be pushed toward God and feel God's love." She acknowledged the limitations of this perspective. "I am not about numbers, which is sometimes unfortunate because sometimes I don't have as big of a vision. But then God makes my vision bigger."

The focus on relationships over numbers can be positive, but it does have some dangers. Andrew, a young missionary involved in campus ministry, explained his experience: "I think we could have done a better job of seeking out more people with whom to build relationships. It was common for us to get trapped into spending time with the same people." He acknowledged his team lacked effectiveness. It was not until some new individuals joined and challenged them that Andrew's team saw its first conversions. He confessed, "People are there who are ready to receive Christ; we just need to find them. I think that we could have done a better job." A focus on investing in relationships without an urgency regarding numbers can result in complacency about seeking out more people to serve. Furthermore, stagnant relationships are less likely to be discontinued and can absorb valuable ministry time and energy.

Marketing

As mentioned in Chapter 2, young leaders value a clear vision that resonates with their values, and they appreciate understanding the purpose behind organizational actions. When churches engage in business-like practices such as marketing, branding, or strategic planning, it is essential that leaders authentically communicate the purpose behind these activities and how they reflect biblical values.

Sara shared her experience being a part of a task force at her church to look at promotion options. "We were comparing ourselves to what another local church does—car magnets, photo contests, giveaways. It's just so bizarre. I realize as a ministry leader you have to raise awareness in your community, but at the same time I was thinking, 'Aren't we just about helping people follow Jesus, as opposed to being the most recognized or visual church in the area?'" The moment business practices appear to take priority over ministry, there is danger of losing the heart of a young leader.

Pastors or CEOs?

Another delicate aspect of the church's adoption of business practices concerns the perception and definition of pastoral and leadership roles. Millennials are often averse to pastoral roles seeming too corporate or formal. While today's young adults value good stewardship and organization, they want the role of a pastor to resemble that of a shepherd rather than a businessperson. One participant shared, "I wasn't questioning the spiritual role of the pastor; I was questioning the institution's implementation of that role, and it felt like a business." He expressed his strong frustration: "If you want to be a business leader, go make some money, but don't hurt God's church." He acknowledged business is valuable, and "we can take some cues from that and not call it ungodly, but we have to be very, very, very careful."

Another young leader shared his experience of applying at a large, affluent suburban church. "They were going to hire me to groom me to be the senior pastor in five years. I asked them why they pursued me. They said they downloaded some of my sermons, liked my blog, and liked my picture: 'You look good.'" He knew then he could not work there. "I thought, 'If I were ugly, but a very gifted man of God, they wouldn't hire me?' I was sensitive to those things." Millennials want the heart, calling, and spiritual giftedness of the pastor to be as important as appearance, popularity, and management and presentation skills.

Leaders and churches seeking to empower and retain young staff members need to recognize that corporate subservience and business models of church governance may fail to motivate, energize, or retain Millennials in ministry positions. So, what models of organization and ministry *do* energize this generation? The following chapter reveals data illustrating the desire of young adults for a relationally strong church, one that functions like a family.

To Millennial Readers

I recently asked a missions leader about the challenges of mobilizing Millennials as missionaries. His observation was profound.

He acknowledged and valued the focus on relationships and discipleship in this generation. However, he saw a lack of passion for and understanding of effective evangelism. While many young adults claim to pursue relationships as a means of demonstrating Christ and his love, some fail to follow through on actually sharing the truth of the gospel with those around them. The question also emerges whether anyone who truly loves God and loves others would not feel an urgency to reach as many people as possible with the truth. What are your thoughts? What is *your* purpose in fostering relationships? Does a focus on discipleship over evangelism result from comfort rather than calling? Why or why not? What are the long-term consequences of the church adopting a focus on relationships over numbers?

REFLECTION QUESTIONS

1. Does your church/ministry/organization experience corporate subservience? How?

2. What priority is given to people versus programs in your church/ministry/organization?

3. How does your church/ministry/organization spend money? What values do you affirm in your spending?

NOTES

1. Dan Kimball, *They Like Jesus But Not the Church* (Grand Rapids: Zondervan, 2007), 83.
2. Peter Haas, "A Church Government Revolution: How to Design a Leadership Structure That Avoids Splits and Enhances Growth," *Substance Church*, February 25, 2008. http://www.substancechurch.com/sites/default/files/files/ChurchGovRevolution-Draft2.pdf. Accessed on October 21, 2013.

CHAPTER 6

Family Priorities

Family is a priority in the lives of most Millennials. While some generations have lived to work, young adults today definitely work to live, and families (in a variety of configurations) represent an important aspect of life. Randy described the tension young adults feel when their work is ministry and it conflicts with family interests. "You never know when the phone is going to ring," he told me. "Your mind is constantly thinking about people at church. It's very hard to balance my home life and my church life. There's really not a clear boundary, so I think the key thing is to make time for your family [and] set aside times during the week for family time." He recognized the importance of his family's role in his ministry. "My wife is very involved in the youth ministry, and that's more beneficial than me being able to work a few extra hours. She gives me a connection to the girls in our youth group that I never would have had, so it's a very good trade-off. And being a dad on top of that, it's a challenge, but it's a lot easier when your family is involved in ministry with you."

In most cases when work or ministry conflicts with a Millennial's life, especially family life, the family wins. Family priorities may include parents, extended family, or close friends, as well as spouses and children. This focus may create tension with colleagues or supervisors who can interpret prioritizing family as a lack of commitment to ministry.

In Loco Parentis

Millennials possess a strong sense of team and a vibrant connection to their families. How Millennials define, understand, and practice family, however, may differ drastically from other generations. This has broad implications for churches hiring or ministering to this generation. Disillusioned by the broken promises of government, economics, and organized church, Millennials value relationships above politics, career, and religion. How Millennials relate to their parents and families of origin, as well as to their own spouses and families, is significant.

Millennials value the role of and connection to parents in their lives as a source of support and encouragement. In some cases, parents may play a significant role in a young adult's decision-making or provide critical support as they adjust to ministry roles or deal with difficult situations. Jocelyn, a young woman serving overseas, described a situation where her supervisor failed to understand this dynamic. She had talked to her mom about a misunderstanding that arose with her missions organization. Her leader later chastised her for discussing the situation with her mother. Jocelyn explained her frustration: "I don't know then who to talk to because my mom feels safe, and she is the type of person who will tell me I need to see it from another perspective. So, who can I talk to?"

Young adults often expect supervisors and leaders to fill a parental role. Millennials value and accept the active involvement of trusted adults in their lives. The helicopter parent phenomenon has received widespread media attention and changed the way many institutions, such as schools, conduct business. In many cases, parents cultivate a close friendship with their children, provide emotional and financial support, defend and protect them, and even promote them to potential educators or employers. Parents of Millennials often work to ensure their children's success, even when it requires personal intervention.

As a result, many young adults desire friendship and mentoring from bosses, leaders, and teachers. This disposition creates a powerful opportunity for those desiring to encourage, empower, and teach the next generation. Millennials also expect older adults who are invested in their lives to protect and promote their best interests, like their parents often did. Unfortunately, parental involvement sometimes impedes the success of young adults. A leader of young adults preparing to enter missions explained that, for some Millennials, dependence on parents actually created barriers and a lack of confidence to pursue ministry themselves.

Sociological historians Neil Howe and William Strauss described the emergence of an *in loco parentis* (in place of parents) doctrine and its projection onto professors, bosses, and other authority figures in the young adult's life.[1] Millennials are extremely responsive to the caring, supportive, parental role in leaders.

Jon explained his relationship with a senior pastor: "I took the effort of maintaining that relationship, and it became a friendship. I felt close to him in that there was more of a relationship there than just working for him. He was my friend. I looked at him almost as a grandfather figure, and he had authority to speak into my life." Randy enjoyed a similar experience with his first senior pastor, describing him as "a very grandfatherly-type guy. You just can't help but love him. He has an amazing heart. When you talk to him for five minutes, you think, this person cares about me. It was very easy to work for him." In her relationship with her pastors, Dana explained she was "working with two special people. We have a very deep, unique parent/child relationship so it doesn't even feel like I am at work. I just feel safe here."

Parenting trends experienced by many Millennials, however, do not necessarily mean healthy family dynamics. Close relationships with parents or families do not always create a sense of stability or safety. As the prominence of traditional families recedes in the United States, many young people have experienced homes affected by divorce, separation, or other difficulties. Even where there is a close connection to parents, the relationship may be lacking the depth, truth, or discipline that can provide emotional stability or a sense of family. If they have not experienced family brokenness themselves, young adults still feel the effects of this reality in the world around them. "My dad taught me," Nick said, but he realized that many young people in his church did not "even have dads; they didn't trust dads." This void created an appreciation for support and parent-like guidance from other significant adults in their lives.

The intense cultural focus on children in the U.S. over the past few decades has often placed them in the spotlight, with parents and other adults watching as they play sports, sing in choirs, or perform in academic and church programs. Millennials have had few opportunities to watch adults and learn life skills. The chance to learn through modeling and mentoring is invaluable to young adults. One study participant described learning from his senior pastor after a death in the church. "I got to walk through the whole process. My senior pastor had me tagging along at all of the meetings to set up the funeral. A lot of those experiences have really helped give me confidence as a pastor."

Another participant explained the difficulty of not learning some lessons earlier in life, saying, "We need to have mentoring and direction." He explained that sometimes young adults benefit from extremely practical advice, such as "When you're in your office, you need to make sure you're doing this, this, this, and this, and you're not just on Facebook and Twitter all day." As the most programmed generation in history, Millennials seldom experienced free time and are used to direction regarding what to do. One young lady preparing to go overseas to serve as a missionary confessed, "I think I am going to need strong leadership to help me set realistic expectations." She explained her tendency to be overly optimistic when setting goals for herself. "I need someone who can set realistic expectations of what ministry is really like when you get out there, because I am going to want to convert the whole city by the time I come home." Young leaders can greatly benefit from intentional coaching from older adults in creating structure and setting goals.

Though many of their interactions with others occur virtually—via texting, social media, and other online means—Millennials value meaningful conversations with leaders in person without a specific work-related agenda, similar to conversations they might have with a parent or friend. Many study participants mentioned getting a meal or coffee with their leader or visiting his or her home, placing value on a relationship outside of a strictly professional role.

When asked what he appreciated about his leaders, Kris explained, "[They were good about] checking in on me and building a friendship with me. We knew things about each other's personal lives, and we hung out with each other outside of work. Not all the time, but it was just a good, healthy balance." This communicated to him that they cared about his well-being, his marriage, and his future. Jacob defined effective equipping of a young leader: "I think it starts with friendship. The person has to know that you care about them and they are not just a tool for the church. That's the hard part, so start with the friendship and out of that will emerge a mentorship." In chapter nine, we will discuss further the critical role of modeling and mentoring in the life of young leaders.

Family First

Investing in one's personal family unit is a priority to many young adults entering ministry. Many Millennials have seen the toll that arduous jobs and long work hours have taken on their parents or families of origin. They have witnessed adults in their lives being laid off from companies after years of faithful service. Entering the workforce during an economic recession, many of them witnessed organizations making deep budget cuts and eliminating many jobs. This has been true not only of corporations, but of the church. As a result, dedication to the company, organization, or church rarely outweighs dedication to one's family.

For Millennials, life comes before work. Family is a part of life viewed as more important than a job or career. Malachi described starting at a new job: "I got here and established a decent rhythm. I give my worst day of the week, Monday, to the church, I don't take that day off. My family gets me on Friday, when I am ready to play. On Monday, I actually spend part of the day reading my Bible, praying, reading books, putting in the spiritual rhythm that I need to be a dad, and a husband, and a pastor." He explained this work/life balance helps him remain effective. "I am ready on the weeks I really have to exhaust myself, rather than living on the bare minimum to the glory of God and then, on the weeks when people really need a spiritual bedrock, being a wasted space."

Leaders who model healthy family relationships earn the respect of young leaders. One young adult described a supervisor she respected. "He would even talk to us about his family a little bit, so we would know his kids when they came in, [and] then you would see him as a dad and a husband. It was fun, because then you could see that side of him, and he wasn't just a boss. We knew enough to make him seem human and approachable." She explained how knowing about one another's families helped develop unity on their team.

Married in Ministry

For those who are married, Millennials' decisions regarding ministry involvement often depend upon how ministry affects their spouse. When a spouse is happy, engaged, or supportive, retention in a ministry role can be much easier. One study participant described how her church helped make the families of staff members feel involved. "When a pastor's wife and kids come by [the church office], we usually drop everything and chat for a while. When people come in, they are the priority."

Jon described the value of a supportive spouse in ministry. "I am blessed with an amazing wife. She's loving, she's caring, and she fills in the details I sometimes miss, which is what you want in a spouse." He explained she is an excellent asset to the ministry and views herself as a pastor as well. "She sees her role as vital, and she sees herself as vital to the church. She's so willing to serve and to help, and that's a good combination for ministry." Malachi shared, "If you have a spouse, I think they need to feel called to ministry too, even though it might look different."

Casey acknowledged that when he has moments of discouragement in ministry and feels he cannot go on, his wife encourages him by saying, "Yes, you can!"

When ministry conflicts with a spouse's satisfaction, desires, or goals, retention becomes much more difficult. In some cases, young adults I interviewed had left their ministry positions to allow spouses to pursue educational or career opportunities, despite their own satisfaction in ministry roles. Some chose to leave ministry when dynamics created a negative experience for the spouse.

One young minister reported a number of factors that made it difficult for his spouse. Demands on his time made it impossible to make plans in their free time. Furthermore, his wife was held to unrealistic expectations. He explained that the paradigm of the pastors he worked with was based on the fact that both husband and wife served on staff full-time. "They're always at the church doing things, and they're unfortunately very much like a typical pastoral family where the church comes before family, or before a lot of things." He remembered feeling at times like his pastors should be at home with their own family. If he had been single, he acknowledged he might have toughed it out. However, it was ultimately more important to get his wife out of that situation than for him to stay there.

Casey started his job as youth minister two weeks after getting married. He and his wife both work in ministry positions now and are happy, but initially, his wife's interests almost led him to leave his position. He explained, "I was here and I was really happy with my job, but I was considering dropping out of ministry because my wife wasn't happy with the jobs she was able to find. She didn't feel like she was accomplishing anything in life. We were starting to have those serious conversations: do we need to move and start applying for jobs in other places where there are more jobs available? I think the Holy Spirit really worked in her being able to find a job she's really happy in and being able to stay here."

Sam echoed the sentiment of many study participants regarding family. "I learned you protect your relationship, your family time; that always takes precedence over ministry. From the get-go, we wanted to protect that." Nonetheless, he explained how the dysfunction at their first church took a toll on his wife. Now, after moving to a different church, "a lot of stuff is healing inside of her, and a lot of passions she had that died are igniting again and so, it's really, really good." Part of the difficulty in Sam's first ministry role was "working for a leader who didn't have a great, healthy home life." That reaffirmed the need for prioritizing family. He noticed, "The healthy family dynamics in the pastor's home overflows into a healthy church staff. If you have a healthy home life, it helps relationships in your churches."

Single in Ministry

Family and relationships also play a significant role in the satisfaction of single young adults in ministry. It may be even more important to encourage time with family and friends for those who do not have the demands of a spouse or children to prompt work/life balance. The words of one study participant illustrate this well: "I think doing it single was another hard thing. I went home and didn't have anyone to talk to about it. I went home and things just brewed inside."

Pastors and leaders can play an important role in encouraging important friendships for young staff members in new ministry roles. Carly explained, "For the first year, your relationships are a mile wide and an inch deep because there are so many people." She remembered her pastor saying, "Let me help you in developing deep relationships, because I know people who will want to go deep with you, but they are not going to be life-giving to you." In doing so, Carly said, "He really helped me a lot." Crystal explained how her pastor really encouraged her to spend time with important friends when the church was going through a difficult time. This type of encouragement can help the young, single staff member navigate the challenges of ministry life.

Single staff members also benefited from connections to families at the church or from having time and freedom to visit or invest in relationships with their own families. Crystal described the connection with her pastor's family: "I spend a lot of time with their family, and I'm just kind of part of the family. It's huge for Pastor Mike to have staff members as part of his family." Carly explained the flexibility she experienced: "When I need to take a day off, I get a day off, especially since I am single and living far away from my family. For every Thanksgiving and every Christmas, I've been allowed to go home." She clarified the impact her pastor's approach has on staff retention. "He wants people to stay for the long haul, so he treats people in a way that makes them want to stay. If you keep staff from their family, they are going to burn out."

Churches and organizations wanting to retain single young adults should recognize and understand Millennials' connections to family and try to facilitate healthy family relationships when possible. Calli, a young adult serving in Asia, described the tension between her peers and their missions agency. "The biggest thing recently was people feeling they need time to go home. They told us at the beginning we would have four weeks to go home or have vacation time, and things have come up where we want to take advantage of that. Now we're told it is only two weeks, where [before] it was four. Then the process we have to go through for getting that decision approved is difficult; our main point person is out of the country two weeks out of every month, and so, we have to wait two weeks to talk to her."

Millennials understand the importance and benefits of maintaining strong relationships with their families. Dana indicated the importance of investing in family relationships: "[If you are in ministry] and don't have good relationships with your family, then you shouldn't be focusing on relationships with other people. It's ironic so many people are in church leadership and their relationship with their actual family is secondary to their church family."

To Millennial Readers

Your value on family represents a great asset of your generation. Not only do you respect parents and grandparents, but you prioritize the needs of your spouses and children. This is definitely an area where other generations can learn from you. Nonetheless, prioritizing family relationships does produce some complications. To what extent do you, and other young adults you know, rely too heavily on the support or encouragement of parents? In what ways do you experience difficulties with developing and exercising appropriate problem-solving and critical-thinking skills? Studies have noted in some young adults a clear lack of understanding of financial realities because of the monetary support they receive from older relatives into young adulthood. How often do you find yourself depending on adults to help you financially or materially? How can you overcome potential barriers to responsible adulthood resulting from family dependence? As Millennials prioritize family, what might be some of the unintended consequences, for better and for worse? What will be the long-term effects on your career, friendships, marriage, and children as a result of perspectives you have adopted toward family?

REFLECTION QUESTIONS

1. What opportunities for mentoring and modeling effective leadership/ministry practices exist in your church/ministry/organization?

2. What measures does your church/ministry/organization take to support healthy work/life balance for staff members?

3. To what extent do individuals working in your church/ministry/organization feel that family is prioritized? Have you asked them? What additional steps could be taken to reinforce strong marriages, families, and friendships for staff members?

NOTES

1. Neil Howe and William Strauss, *Millennials Go to College: Strategies for a New Generation on Campus (2nd Edition)* (Great Falls, VA: Lifecourse Associates, 2007), 3.

CHAPTER 7

Ministry as Family

"I feel like these people are my family, my brothers and sisters, my mom and dad, my grandma and grandpa and uncle," Dana said. Describing the people at the inner-city ministry where she worked, she explained, "To be honest, these people know me at a deeper level than most of my family members do." She saw a profound purpose in working there: "I think God brought me here because it doesn't look like a church is supposed to look, and it doesn't function like it is supposed to function. They are doing something right, and God didn't want me to continue thinking that being a pastor is all about preaching because that is such a very small part. I am realizing you can have a greater effect shepherding through a car ride to the grocery store than from the pulpit week after week."

Dana represents the value Millennials place on authentic community and relationships in a local church or ministry organization. They want to be part of a family. They view the most effective churches as families rather than businesses. For young adults I interviewed, working at a church or organization that embraced their values of prioritizing family and creating a healthy, family-like work environment proved important to job satisfaction and retention. In many instances, however, this vision of ministry as family collides with existing practices of ministry as business.

Dana echoed the sentiment of others when she said, "We use that term *church family* so loosely, but I think if our churches functioned like families, then they would be more healthy and effective. I just want to be a part of churches that look like families." In talking about church, Millennials often desire and define church as people, relationships, or family, juxtaposed against the idea of church as programs, processes, or a corporation. The emerging generation is unlikely to remain satisfied with a church culture that functions largely as a business. As a result, understanding how churches can begin to adapt their practices to current needs is important. In this section, I explain a perspective of church as family, as represented by young adults I have interviewed in a variety of ministry roles over the past few years.

A Family Portrait

Millennials are more comfortable with ambiguity and change than are many from older generations. Sean, a young worship leader, contrasted his perspective with that of his senior pastor: "I know for him, things are just black and white, but for me, there's just a lot of gray, and there's a lot of personal judgment and personal taste and personal conviction. For him, everything is black and white and for me, it's just not." Growing up in an increasingly relativistic culture, many young adults do not see the world structured and defined to the same extent as adults who grew up in a society influenced primarily by modernism and scientific reasoning. While this definitely presents some dangers for the younger generation, it also facilitates adaptability. As a result, Millennials tend to be more willing to embrace the uncertainty and imperfection inherent in a family model of church. One Millennial described her church by saying, "They focus on the people and not the processes, and so everything is messy, but people's lives are being changed."

In a family, individuals often see one another's weaknesses, struggles, and pain. Millennials desire greater authenticity from their leaders and pastors, a level of intimacy that allows for personal connection. One young leader said, "My pastor was so structured, he couldn't be in front or behind that pulpit without being structured. He couldn't communicate relationally; he couldn't tell a story of his own life." Dana explained how her education prepared her for traditional ministry, not for a relational church. "I know how to preach a sermon, but I don't feel like that is intimate at all. Nobody really told me that the way you disciple people is you personally grow with Jesus and then you let people see that growth."

In discussing their philosophies of ministry, Millennials consistently reiterated the concepts of authenticity, intimacy, and safety—characteristic of healthy families. Jesse explained, "We're going to have fun, we're going to laugh, we're going to cry together; this youth ministry will be a family. Part of my vision is just letting students be themselves." Levi described his goal in ministry: "When I lead a small group, I always strive for family. That is obviously not a perfect group of people, but I think it's valuable and I think it's worth it." He explained this meant safety and accountability. "It is loving, but also stretching, and I think it needs to be fun. If it's all business all the time, I wouldn't find it as valuable."

Jesse and Levi represented the views of many of their peers when they emphasized the importance of relationships in ministry. Levi explained, "[Ministry] could be the place where you have some of your deepest relationships. I value family and I think a youth pastor needs to be cool, but also safe enough and family enough to invite and address tough questions." Jesse reiterated, "I know I'm very much a shepherd, and relationships are a big part of the youth ministry." He reaffirmed the importance of people over programs: "It's not going to be an event-driven youth ministry; it will be a lot more about relationships. Maybe it won't always be the coolest, but it's going to be fun, and we're going to build memories together."

For some young adults entering ministry, working through their philosophy of ministry is a process. Balancing conflicting priorities and making choices to invest time and resources in people or programs presents challenges. Carly explained her pastor's philosophy: "His motto always is 'People first.'" Her pastor reiterates to the staff regularly, "We don't run programs; we're about blessing people. I expect you to do a good job at what you do, but people come first." Nonetheless, the pressure to perform is overwhelming. She described having to make deliberate choices to place people above performance. "The more you put people first, you see them respond both to love and relationship. I'm still going to put the time into it, but my lessons don't have as many bells and whistles as when I started, because it doesn't really matter much."

The appeal of a church or ministry team that builds relationships and behaves as family is strong for young people today. One young worship leader described how she decided to accept a position at her church: "They had all the staff over for a meal so I could see how I connected with them, and that's when I felt okay, because I saw how they interacted and they were like a family." In the same way, a church that does not have family elements will struggle to satisfy and retain young adults. One young leader described his church: "The finances of our church are impeccable. It's organized very well. But that doesn't make a church. It was a church that felt like a church, not like a family; nothing was relational, nothing had a personal touch to it."

Supportive relationships are critical for young adults who serve far away from family and friends, especially in their first ministry position. Julie described working with her missions organization: "I would definitely say it's a smaller agency, but that is probably the thing I have liked most about it. I know sometimes it can't offer everything that a big agency can, but I have really enjoyed that it feels like a family." She described what this family atmosphere looked like. "When I e-mail the office, when I e-mail the donations person, I know who it is; it's always the same person; I know her. I like feeling like part of a family. For example, the president knows who I am; I think for me and for now, that's really what I need."

Recently, I talked with a group of young adults preparing to serve in a variety of ministry roles in several different countries. When I asked them what they were going to need to be successful, they overwhelmingly expressed a desire for authentic relationships and community. One young adult echoed the sentiments of the group when she explained, "I feel we are going to need community. For me, honestly it is just about the people around me and solid relationships. I need to know that they are there for me."

Defining church and ministry teams as family may differ from models that intentionally or unintentionally prioritize programs or business. However, the perspectives of young adults can prove valuable in helping churches evaluate their vision for the future. Leadership consultant and author Sharon Daloz Parks believed, "It is unfortunate when the energy of the young adult life is simply resisted and feared as counter to culture rather than prized for its potential as prophetic power."[1] The questions and ideas of young adulthood can encourage consideration for potentially positive changes. So, what changes might be necessary to facilitate better family dynamics in a team?

Family Dynamics

Millennials desire church and ministry teams to function more like a family, but what does that actually look like in practice? They value relationships and programs that allow for a family dynamic or, as some described it, "doing life together." One Millennial discussed living in the community where her church was located and encountering many of the same people regularly: "Seeing people every day and getting to know them on a deeper basis and being known at a deeper level, I have grown in my relationship with God." This depth meant looking at root issues in one another's lives and asking, "How can I help you and how can you help me, and allow Jesus to bring healing mentally, spiritually, emotionally, and physically?" She explained, "I don't just want to be a pastor that feeds the mental part of people. I think there are parts of you that can't be shepherded without deep, deep, doing life together." In her eyes, deep relationships and vulnerability provided a sense of connection and encouraged discipleship and growth.

Millennials preparing to serve overseas discussed the importance of community in their lives. One young adult observed, "To me, community is walking together through life. I am hopeful that as a team we will be able to walk through the ups and downs with each other; to be real and honest and to be able to process what we have experienced in a day and to really grow together through it." Others expressed similar sentiments, indicating a desire for authentic confession, genuine love, and caring accountability. In discussing a potential team, one young man emphasized the need to have a team equipped to build one another up and help each other grow. He believed a strong support system on one's team would allow individuals to go out into the community and make an even greater impact.

Several others described "doing life together." Levi framed it as "being more strategic about connecting people." He also emphasized the importance of accepting the good and the bad that comes along with really getting involved in each other's lives. Nick said, "People always say, 'share life,' but what does that mean?" He believed it entailed people "actually confessing things and holding each other accountable." He saw a lack of this dynamic in the culture around him. "That is our need. We don't know how to do that; we are so isolated and so self-sufficient, we just need to break down sometimes," admitting areas where help is needed.

Ester, a young youth pastor, explained, "For me, discipleship is modeling Christ to other people, letting God's light shine through the cracks of my brokenness and allowing you to be strong in Christ in your weakness as well." She stressed the importance of doing life together as discipleship, emphasizing, "Life continues on when you leave a building, so I would say, going to games and coffee, and making supper and cleaning the house and watching kids . . . those places are really where discipleship happens." The conversations arising out of natural settings and situations in which people were simply doing life together provided unique opportunities for growth. For young adults I interviewed, these various ways of doing life together represented ways of creating a family dynamic within churches and teams.

Facilitating Family

One young man asked, "Just when was it decided, and who decided, that a church service consisted of singing a few songs and then having to sit and listen—bored or not—to someone speak to me for thirty minutes to an hour?" Millennials are tired of church where people attend on Sundays and maybe Wednesdays, and just listen to someone talking at them. Too often, people's lives continue as usual the rest of the week. Millennials long for genuine life change and transformation in the people to whom they minister. They also desire to see those individuals empowered to continue ministry wherever they go throughout the week, rather than relying on pastors to do all of the work of ministry. For many, small groups and intentional community where discipleship and mentoring are occurring help facilitate this growth and empowerment of the entire body of believers.

One study participant explained what happened in small groups at her church: "They revolve around simply getting together and talking about the 'kairos' moments people have each week, because we believe God is speaking to us continually and every week God is doing something new in you." Without intentional community, however, "we don't take time to process through or really evaluate those moments."

Young adults expressed a tension between the time and energy invested in the more traditional church service setting versus that invested in small groups or personal mentoring and discipleship. Nick explained, "I would have gone a more organic route. If it were just me starting this thing off, if I didn't have to work within a system already designed, I would have started with small groups." He acknowledged, "There is an absolute need for the large group, and there's an absolute need for small groups, and the right mixture of that is dependent upon a lot of variables."

Another Millennial youth pastor explained, "We've shifted to a more small-group focus for the youth ministry." He related the benefits of this model. "We deal with issues in the small groups. I think that's probably the thing the kids look forward to the most every week, is spending time in their small group. They really build tight relationships there and I think when visitors come in, they are shocked at what a community it is. Everybody is longing for that." In his ministry, he is seeking a balance between the large group and small group components. "It's really been a change from a more traditional, Sunday morning–type service. We still do all that stuff but it's a lot more condensed, and then we spend time in small groups every single week."

For some, a strong large-group approach to ministry without the supporting family or discipleship component seems irresponsible. Levi echoed the sentiment of others when he reflected on large weekend services without an intentional discipleship component: "It is fine to bring them in, but if you don't have anything to help them grow while they are there, then why even bring them in the first place? Are we really doing them a favor?" Dana explained, "The Bible studies and the great sermons and the choir all play a part, but I think at the same time it's just missing a huge part because if you don't have intimacy, then it's just so shallow."

The difficulty for some Millennials with relying simply on a service to produce growth is that while those settings are effective for conveying information, they do not always develop intimacy and practical application of the information in one's life. Gavin explained, "Information has to be put into some sort of practice. Discipleship is the process of facilitating growth in people and that happens within the context of relationships. I would define growth as people changing, not people gaining information." Nick argued, "We have to be offering what people need, and they don't need to be taught as much as they need to be shown." He admitted, "I was just looking at where we spend our time in church, wondering if our programming was meeting needs."

As a young senior pastor, Malachi adopted an approach to ministry that reflects the values of his generation. "I started trying to identify guys to hang out with. I have a pretty easy discipleship plan: read the Bible and pray with people. I think discipleship is supposed to be easy. Paul says, 'Follow me as I follow after Christ,' so I like to set a pattern of loving people and following Jesus so that if you imitated me, it would help you grow." He described mentors in college who encouraged him to engage in real one-on-one or one-on-two discipleship. As a result, he approached his ministry from the start looking for individuals who were responsive to relational discipleship.

Some young leaders thought larger churches face greater challenges in creating a sense of community and discipleship. Explaining how she enjoys equipping people by just meeting individually with them, Kate lamented one could attend "a 7,000-person church for years at a time and leave not knowing anybody." She acknowledged, "It's not all about community, but community is important, so you've got to have that. And if I look at my life, the relationships with other Christians are what have kept me on track." She felt it should not be as difficult as it often is for Christians to find meaningful relationships in their churches.

Kris served at a large church and concurred. "I think with the large church, the main downfall was a lack of community; you could easily get lost in the crowd." He continued, "That's one of the biggest complaints I heard from people who were in the church and who had maybe attended the church and left. I think even being on staff I could say I sometimes I felt like a bit of a number." Large churches may struggle even more than small churches do to achieve the sense of family Millennials deem to be so essential to personal growth and connectedness.

While values of family and community are vital to intergenerational churches and ministry teams, they extend beyond the church walls. Next, we look at how these values relate to communities outside of the congregations where Millennials serve.

Beyond the Four Walls

Millennials possess a strong sense of responsibility not only to their families, but also to their communities. Their sense of connectedness to others, facilitated through social media and the Internet, along with an appreciation for collaboration and teamwork, create a commitment to social change and justice. When young adults take positions in ministry, they usually bring community-minded expectations into churches and organizations. This extends not only to individuals, but also to other community organizations and places of worship.

Crystal enthusiastically explained her church's desire to invest in their community: "We want to truly be known as a church that serves our community." Of his church, Jon said, "We've got a very high focus on outreach and community service. We're serving downtown once a month; we're serving at a trailer park at least every other month." He also described assistance the church was providing to single moms. This model of ministry to the community resonates deeply with Millennials.

Other young leaders resonated with this desire to serve. Nina explained, "We've been talking a lot about getting outside of the walls of our church and really making an impact with our neighbors. Church is not about coming here to a building. I can get on board with that!" One young senior pastor demonstrated the Millennial comfort with messiness, imperfection, and decentralization for the sake of community, connectedness, and outreach. He explained, "One of our goals is to develop a ministry philosophy for our local body that demonstrates the Great Commission. We encourage our small groups to do outreach of their own. I'd like to decentralize ministry. People in our church recently did some service projects; some tried things and they bombed, but they tried things."

Young adults expressed frustration when a community focus was lacking. Ester explained how her philosophy of ministry differed from the church where she served: "Going into the church, it became very evident the community was not being reached; the vision for the community was really nonexistent." She observed, "When I would talk about things we could do in the community to reach people or reach out, it was very clearly said, 'That is not what our purpose is.'"

Millennials understand the importance of relationships when serving the community. Chelsea, a young adult serving in a community organization in Asia, explained, "The more I got into it, and the more I got to know people, I was like, 'Why would I leave after six months?'" She continued, "I am enjoying it because I understand how it works, because I have relationships. The depth of my relationships is what is going to bring fruit. I can help improve this organization. I am actually an asset, not just a volunteer trying to figure things out."

Extended Family

Many young people serving in ministry become frustrated not only with a lack of relationship with the community, but also the lack of relationship with other churches. Nick described his vision for the church: "There are a couple of huge things on my heart. One of them is unity. I honestly don't know how that's going to happen. That's going to have to be a work of the Lord." His perspectives echo a younger generation's frustration with the politics and disunity among congregations and denominations that reflect poorly on the church. "If we are at all going to stay alive as [the church in] America, we have to show America that Christians are Christians. The church in America will survive if we claim the name of Christ first," Nick asserted. He strongly felt the necessity of collaboration and unity among churches and denominations. "That is the backbone of the church; it has to happen."

Whereas many local churches in the past have operated independent of other faith communities or institutions in their communities, the younger generation believes in the value of seeing these entities work together to improve the common good. Levi described wanting to see more "connecting to other churches in the area" and stated, "It is a shame there is so little of that." He tried to do some joint events with other youth groups while on staff, and speculated in our interview, "[The joint events] probably would have continued, and hopefully on a bigger scale, if I had stayed. I tried to do some of that, but it just wasn't a value of the church."

The Millennial passion for their communities accompanies a sense of responsibility to model the love and unity of Christ to the world. Churches that fail to acknowledge and empower this heart in Millennials may find it difficult to retain them. While Millennials greatly desire the connectedness of family and community, these needs reflect a deeper value of meaningful relationships, especially with mentors and leaders. In the next section, we will discuss these crucial relationships in more detail, depicting their important role in encouraging young adults to pursue ministry and remain faithful to a ministry calling.

To Millennial Readers

The question of who determined that a church gathering should consist of three songs and a thirty-minute sermon is a great one! Answering this type of question requires honest reflection on current practices in the church. However, as we discuss changes to current ministry methods, I have to wonder what questions the next generation of young adults will ask us in another twenty or thirty years as they seek to understand the church. Pastor John Carter wrote a great piece titled "Why Millennials Will Inherit the Earth and Return to the Church." In it he explained, "As a 'revolutionary' it just never occurred to me that my very cool church might not connect with my own kids. I recognize in my Millennial kids many of the same frustrations that I felt as a twenty-something about the evangelical churches I grew up in." He continued, "It is the same hunger I saw in my twenty-something parents that motivated them to leave the mysterious rituals of the old European cathedrals for a vibrant contemporary faith that made sense of the world they lived in."[2] While it is important to bring your perspectives to the conversation about the church, as you do so, consider the answers you will give your kids one day when they ask you about the way you practice church. Believe me, they will ask, and we must be prepared to answer!

REFLECTION QUESTIONS

1. To what extent do you value and model healthy authenticity and approachability? How often do you share personal experiences or struggles as appropriate with team members or staff?

2. How does your church/ministry/organization provide discipleship and mentoring opportunities to encourage personal spiritual growth and accountability? How could you do this better?

3. To what extent does your church/ministry/organization demonstrate unity with other community organizations or churches? What does this look like?

NOTES

1. Sharon Parks, *The Critical Years: Young Adults and the Search for Meaning, Faith, and Commitment* (New York: Harper Collins, 1986), 97.

2. John Carter, "Why Millennials Will Inherit the Earth and Return to the Church," *Fox News*, August 11, 2013. http://www.foxnews.com/opinion/2013/08/11/why-millennials-will-inherit-earth-and-return-to-church/#ixzz2bhxvJ7py. Accessed on October 1, 2013.

PART III

Ministry Needs and Expectations

CHAPTER 8

The Call to Ministry

As a 23-year-old, Jocelyn had been serving in her position for almost a year when I interviewed her. She was working in Asia as a mid-term missionary, striving to help young men and women entangled in the human trafficking industry. Her greatest difficulties upon arriving overseas involved severe misunderstandings with her leaders and confusing expectations from her missions agency. As she shared the hurt, disappointment, and discouragement she experienced as a result, I asked her why she had chosen to stay on the field. She replied, "My missions agency did not call me to Asia. I felt called here by God, and I never felt called out of it!"

Jocelyn shared how she and other young missionaries bonded together in their efforts to overcome obstacles and serve, declaring at one point, "Nobody is going to keep us from doing this!" A sense of calling and community enabled her to stay in the midst of difficulty. Other young adults in ministry echoed the importance of feeling called to ministry. In the next few chapters we will look at various factors critical in the job retention and satisfaction of Millennials in ministry, beginning in this chapter with how Millennials in ministry experience a sense of calling.

Calling to Ministry

Every young adult I talked to during the course of my research shared a story regarding his or her journey into ministry. Most reported experiencing a sense of calling or divine direction to serve in some ministry capacity. Those experiences proved vital to the long-term retention of many in their positions as missionaries, pastors, or church staff members. As we talked, many recognized with surprise the power of recounting influential individuals and moments.

Despite Millennials' significant sense of ministry calling, seldom did supervisors of those I talked to know or understand the background of the young leader's call to ministry beyond a response or two on their job application or in their initial interview. While most ministry leaders possess similar stories, they are seldom discussed or mentioned. A sense of calling draws most of us to ministry and is also the reason why many of us stay. It can also provide a vital connection point for leaders desiring to connect with and inspire a new generation of leaders. As we examine the stories of calling reported by young adults, consider your own story and how often you share it with those you currently lead.

While different for each person, most experiences with calling fall into several categories. These include experience in ministry early in life, a moment or sense of calling, and times of confirmation by important people in an individual's life. Hands-on experience in ministry often leads to a revelation or desire to pursue this work as a career. Others experience an event or moment in which a sense of calling became real or recognized. Several young adults I interviewed cited confirmation or recognition by others as a source of encouragement in pursuing a career in ministry. A couple individuals found themselves in ministry roles by default, as the most logical course to pursue. For some, multiple factors encouraged the choice of a career in ministry. Many young ministers cited calling, regardless of how it emerged, as important to retention and satisfaction once they were in a ministry position.

Prior Experience in Ministry

Active participation in ministry during childhood or adolescence helped develop a sense of competency and passion for ministry in a number of the young adults I interviewed. Carly and her family attended a small church during her childhood and youth. This provided her many opportunities to be involved in ministry, not only at her local church, but also on a traveling team doing programming around the world. She explained, "I found I would rather teach a class of children than even go to youth group." She found a place of belonging serving in the children's ministry at her church. "They needed a lot of help and I just happened to be gifted, and so I naturally fit into those roles."

Several participants grew up in ministry homes, which provided them experience early in life. Nina was the daughter of a pastor. She recounted her experience as very positive. "I grew up in ministry. My parents were very good at keeping the bad away from us as kids, and so I had a very healthy view of the church." She reported being involved in ministry from a young age. "They started plugging me in and letting me use the gifts I had. I was leading worship when I was in youth group and at main services as well. So, it was just a passion of mine God kept confirming through different people." Sanders had a similar experience as the son of a pastor. Early ministry experience revealed his calling to him: "It was just very evident [worship] was something I was great at and something that God had put in my life."

A couple of participants experienced leadership in ministry while still in high school. This experience powerfully impacted their lives and sense of calling. As a teenager, Randy attended a Christian school but did not really connect with his peers. He lived in a small, rural town and really felt he wanted to do something there. When he was about 15 years old, he and a friend decided to start a youth ministry. He explained, "We saw the youth ministry grow from one student our first week to forty kids at one point, and it really made a big impact in that little town." He developed a desire to serve in pastoral ministry. "I felt that calling on my life, and I really have pursued it completely since that point in my life."

Casey described getting involved in ministry during high school: "The church that I was at did not have a youth director, so we would plan our own things. I started to realize I really enjoyed the planning aspect of getting my friends together to do things. That is where the first seed started to get planted of maybe being interested in ministry." The stories of these and others confirmed that doing ministry successfully early in life can lead to a positive inclination toward future ministry involvement.

For other study participants, experience in ministry helped redirect them from other fields into full-time ministry. Previously employed outside the church, Gavin explained, "I took the position [at the church] because they were looking for someone to come in to lead small groups and organize the small-group ministry, and that was something that I had experience with and loved." His passions and desires, discovered through prior ministry experience, aligned with those of the role.

Six months into college, Nick dropped out and started interning with a pastor at his home church. "That was when I decided, I'm going to do it. I don't know how or what exactly, but I'm going to go into ministry." He then went back to school to pursue a degree in ministry. "After that I couldn't stay away. I can confidently say I didn't question my direction at all when I was in college."

Sense or Moment of Calling

While experience serving in ministry resulted in a calling to ministry for some, others experienced a moment of revelation or divine sense of calling that eventually led them into ministry. For young people sensing a call into ministry, an encounter marked by the divine can serve as the beginning of a life dedicated to serving God and others. Ester remembers she was in ninth grade when she first decided to go into ministry. "I had an encounter with God at a Bible camp. God gave me a vision of my high school, and seeing people who were really lost coming to the Lord."

Several others also identified a camp or convention experience as pivotal in their decision to pursue ministry. Crystal explained, "I was just starting my walk with God when I went to a youth camp and heard about being called to ministry, feeling like God wanted to do more with your life and being willing to fully devote your life to him. I didn't even know what that meant, but I knew that was me." Kate described understanding her call to ministry on a missions trip: "I saw evidence of my calling when I was ten. I went on a missions trip and I spoke, and people got saved. I was like, oh, this is it, got it."

For some, the sense of call was disruptive to other plans they had for their lives. Jon explained, "It was definitely God's calling. I wanted to go into the military and then be a police officer. That was my plan, what I wanted to do." As a pastor's son, he had seen negative aspects of ministry and the church. "I liked being in church, but I didn't want to get into church ministry. It really took God pulling at me throughout junior high and high school, calling me, and confirming the call."

Dana also described struggling with a call to ministry: "I felt like I was giving up a huge part of my identity, what I wanted to do. I had wanted to be an interior designer for a really long time." She finally asked herself, "What do you want to spend your entire life doing? Do you want to see the world changed by Jesus' love or do you want to make people's houses look prettier?" Once she made the decision to pursue ministry, she did not question it. "I don't remember where I was, but I remember there was a day I decided that, okay, I'm going to do this. Since then, there hasn't been a question or a doubt in my mind whatsoever."

Growing up, Jacob wanted to be a veterinarian. It was not until college that he sensed a call to ministry. He explained, "When I got to college and had my college pastor mentor me, that's when I began to ask, 'What does church look like? What is the mission of the church?'" In his senior year, his calling was solidified. "I looked at the campus where I was, and so many people were lost and did not know Jesus. I felt the burden for where ministry was going and a call to help." Jacob's sense of calling emerged as he saw the need around him, and was cultivated by his college pastor. He explained, "My college pastor had a big impact; he was my mentor. When he knew I was thinking about ministry, he began to give me opportunities to be in charge of the prayer team and speak, mentoring me in that sense, so that definitely helped."

Confirmation of Calling by Others

For many young people, receiving encouragement and confirmation from adults they respected confirmed their sense of calling. Several young ministers I interviewed received encouragement to consider ministry as a calling and vocation by important individuals in their lives. Jesse related, "I remember my youth pastor telling me all the time, 'You're going to be a youth pastor.'" After taking several ministry classes, Jesse realized he enjoyed it. "I loved it, but still did not feel called. I just felt like I was falling into this backwards because people were telling me that I should do it. Slowly but surely, God revealed different things until I realized, I am called."

For Nina, ministry was something she always wanted to do. In her senior year, an adult shared with her a word of encouragement to pursue ministry, confirming what she was already feeling. That confirmation solidified a sense of calling for her. For Casey, Christian camp counselors made a real impact. He explained, "I kept hearing the same thing from counselors over twelve years, that I should consider working in the church, and that I had natural leadership ability." Later, while in college, these words affirmed a call to ministry in his life.

Jon received ongoing confirmation from leaders regarding his future in ministry. In his role as a youth pastor, he received encouragement from two senior pastors to pursue other pastoral roles in the future. He described a time when his senior pastor said, "Jon will be a senior pastor by the time he is 30." As a result of this encouragement, Jon admitted, "I'm open to it and I wasn't before, but it's taken the last two years of other people saying it for me to get to the point where now I'm open."

Malachi encouraged young people considering ministry to seek out confirmation from trusted individuals in their lives. "Find mentors who are spiritually whole and submit to what they have to say in your life. Ask them, 'Do you think I can do ministry?'" He also acknowledged, "A lot of guys go into ministry before anyone has put their hand on them and said, 'I think God has a call on your life.'" In the next section, we will look at such individuals, who entered ministry but did not indicate a particular sense of calling.

Ministry by Default

Some individuals find themselves in ministry roles somewhat by default. The lack of a specific sense of calling can affect ministry retention to the inverse degree that a *strong* sense of calling can support retention. Levi explained, "I was a ministry major. My dad's a pastor so I just always thought that's what I would do. I understand the culture of church, I understand being in a ministry family, and so it just makes sense." Nonetheless, when it came time to graduate and pursue a position, he admitted, "Towards the end, I don't think I wanted it as much, but it seemed like the natural thing to do." After a brief time on staff at a church, Levi no longer serves in church ministry.

After graduating from college, Sean got a full-time ministry position immediately. He explained, "It was the easiest job for me to get; it just kind of fell into place right when I needed it and so I went for it." He described not feeling any hesitation about the position and feeling like it was what he needed at the time. He did not feel the compulsion to pursue ministry that others described. "I had never said, 'I want to do this; this is what I want to be; this is what I think I am supposed to be.' The pieces fell together for that place at that time." He too served for a brief time in that initial ministry position and then went on to pursue other career opportunities.

The Value of Calling

The importance of a call to ministry emerged repeatedly throughout my conversations with young adults. Carly said, "Make sure the Lord has called you to ministry, because when things get hard, you are going to have to look at that calling and know to stick it through, because that is what you are supposed to do with your life." Gavin reiterated this message: "Make sure this is what God's called you to do. If God's called you, it's for a reason; [God's] going to give you strength and what you need to be successful." Others agreed that calling is essential for long-term endurance in ministry. Sam warned, "Don't get into youth ministry or ministry just because someone you loved growing up did it and you want to be like them. You better know God called you to do it."

Crystal shared a powerful story of her church going through a period of turmoil and difficulty. When her pastor talked to her about the situation, she responded, "Pastor, I'm called here. I will do whatever I have to do. If I have to go get another job to support myself in ministry, I'll do it because I am called here." She further explained, "There are a lot of times it would have been so easy to say, 'I'm done!' But I know that's not what God has called me to do."

Malachi offers advice for young people going into ministry. "I think what my pastor told me is true: if you can do anything other than full-time ministry, you probably should. Like Paul, you should feel compelled [to be in full-time ministry]." He explained his own heart for ministry: "I felt that sense of compelling. I care about other churches and future pastors already as a young pastor. I want to be the kind of man that can offer something to a young pastor."

Jacob expressed the importance of ministry leaders hiring individuals who know they are called to full-time ministry. In order to understand someone's sense of calling and encourage it, we must ask about it. As we do so, we must also be willing to share our own stories. Understanding the God-ordained experiences of those around us fosters respect, trust, and understanding. While a sense of calling is foundational to job satisfaction and retention in ministry, several other factors also greatly impact ministry experience for Millennials. These include relationships with leaders and colleagues, identification with the vision of the ministry, and a sense of effectiveness in their roles. In the next chapter, we will look closely at the relationships young adults have with supervisors and peers in their ministry roles.

To Millennial Readers

What is the story of your call to ministry? Who or what has affirmed that calling over the years? What were or are your motives for pursuing your current ministry position? Take time periodically to reflect on these questions. Also, consider the frustrations or trials you are facing today in your ministry position. What is the source of those struggles? Do they negate your calling? Why or why not? Consider what you need to change or the help you need to seek to remain faithful to your calling. Make a list of attitudes and actions you need to address. If necessary, write down what you need from your leaders or colleagues to be successful in your ministry position. Discuss those topics with them and ask them for honest feedback.

REFLECTION QUESTIONS

1. When was the last time you reflected on your call to ministry? How have you been faithful to that call?

2. How often do you ask those around you why they decided to pursue ministry? How often do you share your story with them?

3. When have you taken the time to affirm the calling or gifts of others recently?

CHAPTER 9

Vital Relationships

"It was just very, very hard at times," Sean said of his first ministry position. "Pastor James and I didn't always see eye to eye, and we didn't always understand each other. He didn't understand where I was coming from, the mind of a 23-year-old."

He explained the unraveling of their relationship after an incident in which they saw things differently. "I was in his office and he was getting frustrated that I wouldn't talk about it. I tried to say, 'Pastor, I just don't have anything good to say right now, and I need to let my personal feelings die a little before I can talk to you about this in a good manner.'" His senior pastor adopted the approach of a boss, Sean explained. "He kept pushing me and pushing me and pushing me until finally, he just slammed his hands on his desk and said, 'I am your boss. You sit down and talk to me right now.' That was when I realized we really couldn't work well together and it just fell apart; it fell apart." Within a few months of that incident, Sean left his position at the church and he no longer works in ministry.

Leaders

Leaders play a crucial role in the retention and success of young adults in ministry. Millennials desire and expect relational leadership from their senior pastors and other leaders. It is important to understand what this looks like in practice. When leaders view ministry as a business, they often see their role as that of a boss. As discussed earlier, many young adults desire the church to function more like a family. This brings with it the expectation of leaders being approachable, personal, and caring. Leaders who make the effort to be a friend or mentor, as well as a supervisor or manager, have the greatest opportunities to invest in young leaders and impact them for future ministry effectiveness.

As I interviewed young adults in ministry, the quality of their relationships with leaders was quickly apparent. Those with strong, supportive relationships tended to thrive. Jon explained, "I have a pastor who supports me and cares about me, and that more than anything has helped me to stay." Talking about her pastors, Dana described, "I've just never met anybody like them and never had a relationship like I've had with them, and it's changed who I am and the way I live and the way I view things." In contrast, those who felt misunderstood, unsupported, disregarded, or disempowered by their leaders expressed frustration and discontent in their positions. Let's look at some of the key factors in empowering relationships for Millennials in ministry.

Accessibility

There are a number of qualities that facilitate healthy and thriving relationships between young staff and their leaders. One of them is accessibility. In describing his first year of ministry, Levi acknowledged, "It was a very isolating time." Isolation or disengagement can result from the absence or inaccessibility of the leader. Levi explained, "Pastor Bradley made some of the final decisions, but he was very rarely in the office. He would be out, doing I don't even know what." In meetings, Levi's senior pastor "would often be up walking or messing around or on his computer or whatever, so he was never really engaged."

Gavin explained, "As far as Pastor Andy, there being a connection there, there wasn't. Half of the time he wasn't even at the weekend services and if he was there during the week, he was in meetings. He wasn't there during the week to be part of the staff." The fact that his pastor "always seemed very busy" dissuaded Gavin from simply approaching and talking to him. Others I interviewed reported various reasons for inaccessibility of senior leaders. Sean described his pastor having many outside commitments. Others felt their pastors had personal issues, resulting in choices to remain distant from the church and staff.

One young leader admitted feeling some bitterness in regard to his pastor's inaccessibility and the nature of their relationship. "I think I learned a good lesson. Whoever you are reporting to, it's going to be a working relationship. I wish I would have known that beforehand." He explained how he sometimes felt his pastor didn't care about him. He acknowledged that when they were able to connect, his conversations with his pastor were meaningful and helpful. The irregularity of these interactions, however, proved disappointing.

In some cases, young leaders intentionally remained disconnected from leaders. Kate explained, "I never quite joined his team because I could see a lot of abuse happening in the way he and his wife treated people who did come under them, and I was not about to participate in that." Another participant explained that his pastor, who was also his direct supervisor, took little time to understand his job. "He maybe knew 20 percent of what I was actually doing. Whenever I had a meeting with him, I always had to set it up and say, 'Can I meet with you sometime today?'" He further acknowledged, "If I had something going on in my personal life or if I was struggling with something, I wasn't going to go talk to him about it." This sense of disconnectedness produced isolation and left the young leader feeling unsupported in his role.

Support and Trust

A sense of being supported and trusting one's leaders contributed significantly to ministry effectiveness and retention for the young leaders I interviewed. Randy said, "I think the most important thing leaders need to do is believe in you—believe in your vision and be supportive of you." Carly described arriving at her first full-time ministry position: "It was hard at first, because people were used to a really different style then mine. But, because Pastor Paul trusted me and they trusted him, people did not question me in the things I did."

Young leaders indicated feeling supported when they knew their leaders trusted them, even in the face of difficult situations. Kris explained, "My leaders all had my back. If a situation came up where it meant a family or two leaving the church or [me losing] my job, I knew I wasn't going to lose my job over it." As a result, he explained, "I felt free to stand up for what I felt was right."

Jon also conveyed how his pastor supported him. "I never had to worry about getting into a situation where somebody was accusing me of something." He described being trusted by his leaders. "That's been reaffirmed this week in a situation that's going on in the church. Pastor Matt has been very supportive and encouraging and not condemning. It'd be easy for him to have handled it differently, but I walk away and I know I've got a pastor who supports me and cares about me." Jon acknowledged the blessing of his situation. "I've been fortunate, because I know other pastors and other youth pastors aren't in situations like mine. So for me, it's been a blessing [that] I've had my leaders' trust and I've trusted them."

Dana described how a close and trusting relationship with her pastors helped overcome other obstacles that arose. "Pastor Alex is as opposite as you get from me, on so many levels—work style, personality style, thinking style, communication. He is a major extrovert and is managing a lot of different people. Then there is me, who has all her ducks in a row and has her weekly schedule planned out." She indicated the impact that trusting and following her leaders had on her life: "God has given me the ability to just trust them and be their follower, and they've changed my life and have played a really irreplaceable role in shaping me."

Andrew, a young leader serving in Africa, described the support he received from his leaders and missions organization. "They really do care about the people they send, and they have a really good support network and system set up. The people I worked with took the time to take care of me." He explained the different ways support was provided. "The wealth of resources was really nice, anything you need to know about why you are there, about the culture, about anything. They have a strong emphasis on learning the culture and on having nationals who are in leadership, which I think is extremely valuable. I just really appreciated that."

Other young leaders described the detrimental effects of ministry leaders and organizations who failed to support them effectively. As mentioned in Chapter 3, Millennials choose whom they will follow. Leaders and organizations that appear unworthy of trust will find it difficult to empower or influence the next generation.

Lindsey, a young woman serving in Asia, described communicating with her missions organization regarding an issue that came up. "I tried to communicate this was something very important to my team. I asked them to take time to listen to our needs, take time to restructure this program so it was something that worked. The message I got back was, 'Just trust us.' I told them, 'How can we trust you when you haven't given us any reason to trust you in the last year and a half?' They still don't understand that. I just got back the answer, 'You need to submit to our authority; you need to stop asking questions; you need to trust us.' That is not the answer we need to hear. . . . Whether in a friendship or an organization, trust must be earned."

After serving in ministry overseas for almost two years, Lindsey concluded, "Your sending organization should support you, understand your needs, and be readily available to talk to you if you are having problems." She emphasized that the support needed was more than just a business relationship, but rather someone to talk to when difficult situations arose. "I think there should be individual coaches for each person. Member care needs to be high on the list of values for missions agencies, and it's not right now."

Connie served overseas as well and experienced a lack of support from her leaders on the field. "My team leaders connected more with my teammate, and I was kind of the odd one out. That was really stressful. I didn't have any support group, so I was getting really worn down." The way her leaders and sending organization handled her first year on the field created a lot of confusion for her. "I'm very distrustful of missions organizations now. I don't feel released from the people God has put on my heart, but I realize how people will let you down, and that I cannot rely on people. I can only trust God." Connie now lives and works in the United States, despite her desire to work overseas.

Empowerment and Freedom

Young adults reported experiencing empowerment from their leaders and colleagues in two ways. The first was experienced as freedom to be creative and make honest mistakes without punitive consequences. This is especially important when Millennials feel pressure to achieve and thus place inordinate pressure on their own performance. The second important element of empowerment was the ability to have a voice and vision. Nick referred to this as "whiteboard rights" or the ability to "scribble all over," giving input and having ownership in the ministry. Most Millennials experienced empowerment and freedom as positive, except in instances where they felt an absence of feedback and support.

Many young leaders voiced an appreciation for the freedom to make mistakes. Dana explained, "I mess up a lot; it's really hard to work in ministry sometimes. I know there are different areas where I don't meet expectations, but Pastor Alex never focuses on those at all. He does not scold me and tell me what I did wrong, because he knows I am aware; he's just like, it's okay. So, that makes our ministry a place where I can learn. I'm experiencing a lot of growth on my own from being able to learn and mess up and then do things over."

Nina described her staff as having "freedom to be who you are." She continued, "You can try anything once, and then if it doesn't work, try it differently. I think that dynamic is really healthy." Kris described a similar freedom on his team where mistakes became opportunities for learning and staff could try new things in a responsible way. Several individuals cited supportive bosses as essential to feeling freedom to make mistakes, learn, and grow as young leaders. They also appreciated opportunities to dream and pursue their vision for ministry. When she applied for her position, Carly asked, "How much freedom are you going to give me?" It was very important to her to know she would be able to implement her vision.

Remember that Millennials have grown up in a culture where everything has been programmed or supervised for them. Therefore, when young adults are given freedom, they must also receive the support to empower the implementation of their ideas. Gavin experienced the freedom to make decisions and implement ideas, but struggled with the lack of support he received. "They definitely empower you to make decisions and expect you to be able to come up with ideas on your own. It's very hands-off: this is your department, and this is what we expect from you; do it, or figure out how to do it." While he appreciated being empowered and provided with ample resources, he did feel the lack of support and feedback. He wondered if after thirty years of ministry, his leaders didn't want to train or coach someone young, but rather needed someone to waltz in and run the ministry without requiring any support.

Millennials expect the same empowering leadership they strive to give. Ana explained what she valued in leading her ministry team: "Knowing my team, knowing their strengths and weaknesses and helping them, pushing them. Sometimes they don't even know what their dreams are, so my role involves pushing them, investing time in them, praying and trying to figure out what God has for them." She also described how she supported those working with her by "spending time with them, praying and caring for them."

Ana went on to define the leadership needed for her generation: "If people see us for who we are, we will flourish. We want to be trusted. Even in the mundane tasks, if people validate that we do them well, we will continue. We need pastors to listen to some of our dreams and care about how we are going to reach them. They don't have to babysit us; we can Google how to achieve our dreams, but Google won't listen to us and say, 'Oh, that is a good idea—now do it.'" Most young adults have passion, but also benefit from relationships, resources, and personal feedback in implementing their vision.

Friendship and Personal Connection

Jacob defined his view of leadership: "I think it starts with friendship; the person has to know that you care about them and they are not just a tool for your church." He explained that building a friendship with staff can be difficult for senior pastors and leaders. After serving as a young minister at five different churches, he admitted he had only experienced a friendship with a leader in one instance. He referred to others who had experienced a personal relationship with leaders: "I have heard of people who have gotten to be under that kind of leadership and mentorship and it makes a huge difference; they succeed." He acknowledged the challenges inherent in this philosophy of leaders as friends. "I understand where pastors are coming from; they are just so busy. We make church these days so full of programs that we don't have time [for relationships]."

For many young leaders, a friendship and relational connection with senior leaders emerged as a powerful factor in personal and ministry development. Jon explained his relationship with his senior pastor, saying, "I made it a rule, whenever he invited me out to lunch, to go. Even if I had a lunch, even if I didn't have money for lunch, I just went because he was a very wise man with a lot of experience." His relationship with his senior pastor developed into a friendship. "I took the effort of maintaining that relationship, and it worked in my favor. He had so much wisdom for me and so much counsel. The relationship began to blossom; it was not just a leader/subordinate relationship. Pastor Matt was my friend. He had authority to speak into my life."

Many others expressed the value of a personal relationship with their leaders. Related Kris, "[I appreciated my leaders] just checking in on me and building a friendship with me. We knew things about each other's personal lives, and we hung out with each other outside of work . . . not all the time, but it was just a good, healthy balance." Of his leaders, he said, "[They made a] personal investment; they cared about me, about my marriage, about my finances. They took time to make sure I was spiritually, emotionally, physically healthy." He saw their impact on his life as long-term. "In developing me as a pastor, they helped me to fulfill my lifelong call to do ministry. That was huge." Relationships with invested leaders contributed to a sense of effectiveness in ministry roles. I consistently heard young leaders express the benefits of close, personal, encouraging relationships with senior leaders and other older adults who served as mentors or role models.

Mentors and Role Models

In many cases, significant mentors and role models have played a vital role in the ministry effectiveness and personal growth of young leaders. These relationships have sustained Millennials in ministry roles where the leadership was unsupportive or nonexistent. Modeling also provides young adults a valued and longed-for opportunity to learn from those with more experience. Modeling can often take the form of mentoring. Writing about what inspires young people to dedicate their lives to serving others, researchers Laurent A. Parks Daloz, Cheryl H. Keen, James P. Keen, and Sharon Daloz Parks explained, "People tend to be drawn to mentors who know and have experienced something that they sense they need to learn."[1] They respect those adults and leaders who are consistent in modeling the ideas they promote.

Doug, a young senior pastor serving in a small town, expressed the importance of his relationship with another pastor in a nearby town. "He has played a huge, huge role in my life. He has been in ministry for over twenty-five years now, and he is a lot like me. The way I am now is a lot like he was when he started, so we have made a great connection and he has been a great help." Doug also received support from other pastors in his denomination. "Our region has formed leadership communities, and I meet once a month with a group of pastors. We study a book, do accountability. That group has played a part in my journey of self-discovery and self-reflection."

Another young senior pastor, Malachi, described working in a previous position as a youth pastor. "There was a youth pastor nearby in his mid-50s, and I would call him quite regularly and we would meet and he would do some coaching." He described another key individual in his personal and ministry development. "A staff member from the parachurch organization I was once involved with has always been a mentor from afar, regarding what it means to lay the foundation for ministry for the long haul. It is amazing what mentors do to protect you and to steer you." Malachi further described choosing a seminary to attend based on the mentoring that was provided. "When I read about their mentoring program and their insistence upon learning to be someone who grows, I knew that was a good fit."

Jacob described the influence of his college pastor as both a role model and mentor in his life. "He was a guy who, going back to the Greek way, had *pathos*, passion; *logos*, knowledge; and *ethos*, ethics. Here was a person who, as he got up to speak, had a passion, and you knew he believed what he was preaching. He was someone who taught you something, and then he lived it too." He described the mentoring relationship that emerged: "We met probably once a week or every two weeks. We became friends in a mentoring sense."

Young adults serving in ministry roles overseas, far from family and friends, also stressed the need for mentorship. Lindsey explained, "I had a lot of expectations our missions agency would provide more spiritual mentorship, mentorship adjusting to the culture and being away from home, and emotional and spiritual support. I thought it was inevitable that they would keep us accountable, and I didn't realize you as an individual are responsible for that. If you need it, you have to ask." She explained that a mentor or coach back in the States would be helpful, but also wished for someone more local: "It would be a huge help if there were a middle-aged person here on the field who was kind of our coach."

Julie benefited from a mentorship program being in place when she arrived on the field for her first missionary assignment. "Our missions agency has really thought a lot about this program and the fact that we are going to come over and be mentored by older missionaries who have been on the field. I think it's really important your first time to have that because I would have been lost if I had no other experience in missions."

Colleagues and Teams

Julie also expressed the importance of being involved on a missionary team. She is not alone. Many Millennials find relationships with teammates or colleagues to be very important to their growth and success. In fact, healthy team dynamics have contributed significantly to the job satisfaction and retention of Millennials in ministry roles. Jon said of his church, "You come to work and you want to be here. I like the people I work with; we support each other, we pray for each other, we walk through life together."

Crystal and Carly both reported a sense of family and connectedness on their teams. Crystal explained, "I haven't experienced anything else, so I don't know, but our staff really enjoys being together. Our lead pastor is extremely relational, and from his perspective, if we don't have fun doing ministry together, we should not be doing ministry together." Carly described, "We treat each other like family. Every morning, when we first come in, we try to take ten or twenty minutes to socialize with the office staff and connect."

For Connie, relationships with other missionaries provided support as she prepared to go overseas. "It was really good to be with a group of people who were going through the whole fundraising process at the same time. We met and checked in with each other. I was kind of on my own, but knowing I wasn't alone was really nice."

Isolation and discouragement can occur through a division of labor or lack of interaction with other staff. One young man reported, "I was the only person who was concerned about discipleship. Maybe saying I was the only person is a little bit extreme, but there weren't many other people I worked with in that area. I was disconnected from everything that was happening." Ester felt the same dynamic in her role: "I felt very disconnected from the rest of the team. I felt pretty disconnected from other ministries in the church. I didn't really feel like I had a role in things, even though I was a part of the staff there. Our team never met together; we never had any discussions together." Levi explained the isolation he experienced: "I would come in on Monday morning and I was the only one there, and I would spend most of that day just working on website stuff."

Relationships are crucial to the success of young adults in ministry roles. One or two vital relationships can sustain them through significant challenges. Today's leaders seeking to empower and influence the leaders of the future must find ways to foster healthy relationships with their followers, as well as create an environment for effective team relationships. In the next chapter, we will look at other significant communication skills for leaders working with young adults.

To Millennial Readers

More than other generations, you value healthy, thriving relationships. Proverbs 18:24 talks about different types of friends and their impact on our lives: "Some friends play at friendship but a true friend sticks closer than one's nearest kin" (NRSV). As you look to grow and flourish in ministry, pursue those friendships that are reliable and life-giving. Also, remember that effective relationships are a two-way street. Take the time to consider the type of friend you are to those on your ministry team. Do you sacrifice and serve to empower your leader's vision, or do you simply look for encouragement in your own goals? Do you genuinely care for and encourage your leaders and teammates? If you see ruin in relationships around you, consider any unreliable characteristics in your own approach to friendship. Develop the heart and traits that allow you to serve and care for others humbly and lovingly!

QUESTIONS FOR REFLECTION

1. What elements of friendship or personal connection exist between leaders and subordinates in your church/ministry/organization?

2. How many people would call you a mentor or role model? Why?

3. To what extent do individuals on your team enjoy working with one another? With you?

NOTES

1. Laurent A. Parks Daloz, Cheryl H. Keen, James P. Keen, and Sharon Daloz Parks, *Common Fire: Leading Lives of Commitment in a Complex World* (Boston: Beacon Press, 1996), 45.

CHAPTER 10

Communication of Vision and Value

"It became almost like a country club," Jacob said as he reflected on a church where he served. "We got together for relationship, but we didn't know what our mission was; we didn't really invite anyone or have a purpose, other than calling ourselves a church. We had our little get-togethers, our small groups, but we were not really involved in outreach, evangelism, or discipleship."

According to Jacob, a Millennial youth pastor, leaders need to be "passionate for the kingdom [of God] and have a clear vision that we are a church and are called to expand his kingdom." While healthy relationships contribute significantly to the development and effectiveness of Millennials in ministry, relationships are not enough to inspire and empower young adults for long-term commitment to a team or organization. Leaders hiring young leaders can maximize the retention and empowerment of this generation by embracing a clear vision and communicating the value that young leaders add to the pursuit of that vision.

Communicating Vision

In defining leadership, Kris said, "It's ordering, delegating, and being willing to recognize your vision and stick to it. It's realizing the vision is bigger than just one person." He also emphasized the importance of hiring individuals whose vision aligns with the leader and organization. "I think it is important to make sure people agree with the vision of your church before you hire them. Make sure they understand what it is you are trying to do and see if their way of doing ministry lines up with that."

Millennials are a diverse group, and at times the perspectives articulated by this generation regarding the church seem contradictory. As a result, it is essential that churches and organizations hiring young adults clearly articulate their vision throughout the interview and hiring processes. It is better to discover a conflict in vision before individuals are hired than to deal with the resulting frustration once they are on staff. Furthermore, Millennials quickly disengage when working either in an environment lacking vision or for a leader who appears directionless.

Vision must not only be articulated but integrated into practical aspects of the organization. Malachi would ask his senior pastor, "What is the vision of the church?" Malachi explained, "I have to know what I am supposed to be doing here. Give me the vision, and I will submit." When his pastor proved unable to communicate a vision, Malachi eventually left that ministry role. Sam explained, "We always talk about having vision, and I think every pastor has a vision, but not every pastor is good at working to make it happen." His church had a stated vision, but nothing occurred to propel that vision forward. He differentiated, "There's vision and then there's diligence to make that vision a reality." Sean echoed similar frustrations. He described the vision at the church where he previously worked as admirable, but admitted, "They were not accomplishing it in the slightest. Things weren't being done with excellence or full commitment."

A perceived lack of follow-through or action on stated goals, and no clear measure of success, produces frustration for many young adults. One worship leader explained, "My pastor would promise me so many things about where this church was going and the vision he had, but nothing ever happened." Jesse said, "I was told, 'You can do whatever you want; the sky is the limit. If you dream it, just do it.' And then I'd get an idea and they'd say, 'No, no, we're not going to do that.'" His pastor's expectations confused him. "I felt like he had the vision and I didn't know exactly what it was supposed to look like, so I was either going to stand still or just do whatever [I wanted], but probably not what he wanted." Unpredictability contributed to Gavin's feelings regarding the vision of his church. "It seemed like everything changed from one meeting with Pastor Andy to another, so it was very confusing to figure out what we were doing."

Participation in the development of the vision encourages ownership by young adults. One young leader discussed how she valued contributing to the vision process at her church. "When I first came in, they were going through our mission statement, reworking it, which was good for me, coming in new. I was able to be a part of all those conversations." She described advocating for certain ideas to be included. When her ideas received consideration, she was able to buy into the vision and take ownership. She explained, "It wasn't just about a statement, but it was about what are we actually doing, and who do we believe we are supposed to be, and what does it take to get there?"

Not only does participation encourage engagement, but it also helps Millennials understand the challenges of developing and implementing vision. Unique difficulties exist for large or international organizations in ensuring consistency between articulated vision and the implementation of that vision. Repeatedly, I hear frustrations from young adults serving overseas with missions agencies or international relief and development organizations.

After hearing a moving presentation, talking to a mobilizer, or perusing a website, Millennials apply and go to serve in a specific capacity. However, from the time they sign up to when they arrive on site, things change. Sometimes a lack of communication between home offices and field workers results in misrepresentation of what is actually occurring. Perhaps because young adults are accustomed to receiving updated information regarding any topic of interest instantaneously via a news feed, an e-mail alert, or a text message to their phone, it is often difficult for them to grasp the complexity of international work. In these instances, it is important for young adults to understand clearly the potential for change or nuances in how the vision of the organization applies in different cultural contexts. When presented as a challenge and adventure for those who are adaptable and called, the right individuals will respond to this type of experience.

One valuable tool for the working out of vision, regardless of location or context, is regular team meetings. When meetings lack a clear vision or purpose, however, this can also be a common trouble area for many teams and organizations. Randy explained his pastor's philosophy was to "brainstorm and talk during staff meetings." However, Randy described his own preference: "[I tend to] come in with a plan and make the best use of our time." Sam echoed this sentiment: "One of the toughest things for me was the weekly staff meeting, which was 90 percent talking and hanging out. I have a very driven personality, and the weekly staff meetings were something I dreaded." Ester also expressed frustration with the mundane, directionless conversation that dominated most staff meetings with her senior pastor. She described finding these meetings unproductive and a waste of time.

As we will discuss further in the next chapter, young adults want a meaningful work experience. When a vision exists and they can contribute to its development or implementation, they feel ownership. Leaders who fail to encourage and activate a shared vision lose credibility and may appear dishonest and undependable to young followers.

In many ways, young adults' expectations of vision contain great irony. They expect from others the very behaviors they often struggle to adopt. While many young adults feel passionate about specific causes or initiatives, few can actually articulate a clear vision for their own involvement or implement a successful strategy to achieve goals. Nonetheless, working with effective leaders and teams to develop and implement vision can help them gain these invaluable skills.

One of the most important elements Millennials bring to a vision process is awareness of new ideas and trends in culture that can help inform a vision for the future. They want a vision that makes sense in the world they see and live in daily. They understand that challenges face the church they will be leading in the days to come. Integrating a vision for today with a vision for the future can help bridge intergenerational perspectives.

Despite the relativism that informed much of their education, many of the young adults I interviewed discussed the challenges they perceived for the church and their desire to see truth incorporated uncompromisingly in ministry. Ana described her frustration. "We try to look like the world. We try to have all this media and draw people in, instead of just looking at the Bible and giving people the Bible with life, and giving people Jesus." She explained, "Sometimes I think the church tries to apologize for being biblical, living according to the Bible. If you compromise, Millennials are going to write you off because you are not being true to what Jesus says."

Jacob echoed similar sentiments. "I think the biggest challenge is getting some churches to put the gospel back at the center and to keep it there—not getting caught up in so many trends of what the church is supposed to look like and following those trends." He explained one of the difficulties of working as a youth pastor today. "Young people don't understand that truth is truth and we can't have two contradictory truths." Ben acknowledged that much of the current friction in the church, often between generations, revolves around the ideas of truth and grace. He said our challenge consists of "finding that balance between God's grace and God's truth and working together in that."

Communicating Value

While Millennials respect leaders who embrace truth and pursue a clear vision, they also desire affirmation that their contributions to that vision are valued. Leaders of Millennials can maximize the retention and empowerment of this generation by consistently communicating the value young leaders add to the pursuit of a team's or an organization's vision. While this may feel like hand-holding to some in the older generations, it is important. As discussed in

Chapter 2, young adults today have many options. A Millennial who feels called and desires to make a difference in the world can search the Internet and instantly find thousands of positions with churches, nonprofits, government organizations, or community programs. Leaders hoping to retain the talent and energy of young leaders on their teams must provide consistent communication and feedback to these individuals, affirming the value they bring to the goals and vision of their church or organization.

Feedback and Affirmation

Millennials value honest, sincere communication. Leaders who provide affirmation and correction out of authentic love and concern for the young adult convey value and earn the right to be heard. Young leaders benefit greatly from constructive feedback. Kris explained how his leaders would give him feedback after sermons and programs. "There were a couple of times where I messed up and they let me know about it, but it was done out of love, and that made all the difference."

Carly explained her pastor's approach to leadership. He told her, "If I ever have a problem with something you do, I'm going to tell you immediately. You never have to worry that I am upset with you or I am disapproving of something, because if I am, then I'll tell you." She described the relief associated with not having to wonder where she stood with her boss.

Because Millennials truly desire to please those they trust and respect, effective leaders will find ways to encourage young staff. Remember, this generation has been conditioned to receive a gold star or trophy just for showing up and participating, so an absence of affirmation communicates something is wrong. When her pastor asked Nina if she needed more feedback, she responded, "Yes! If I don't hear what you are thinking, I automatically assume something negative. If I don't get any encouraging words, I automatically think I've done something wrong." Thus, feedback not only encourages but also contributes to the ability of young leaders to serve confidently.

Relationship and Responsiveness

Whereas affirmation from a leader can meet the deep need Millennials have for feedback, listening and responding to them can create a sense of accessibility, trust, and respect for the leader as someone who truly values the perspectives of others. Millennials respect leaders who can listen and *receive* honest feedback graciously. Ester explained, "I think a good leader is an active listener." She acknowledged the importance of a leader who genuinely considers and responds to input from others. Leaders who fail to listen and communicate effectively with Millennials jeopardize any opportunity to influence or empower them. As we see in the following examples, communicating that young leaders are valued by leaders and organizations requires both relationships and responsiveness.

Lindsey described communicating with people at her missions agency. "I wish that we had been given time to get to know the people at the agency because I found in communication that, if you don't have a foundation of a friendship with them, it is hard to have grace with them, especially in e-mail." Because so much communication today occurs electronically, more intentional effort must occur to facilitate relationships. Lindsey acknowledged, "It is hard when you don't know a person's communication style or personality. I have a lot of grace with my teammates because I know them, but we can't really do that with people at the agency. It's been hard to get to know them over Skype; it feels really business-like and not personal."

One of the most important elements of effective communication with young leaders is timely responses. They are accustomed to immediate feedback, and timeliness in responses is critical, especially via e-mail, texting, Facebook, or other social media venues. Lindsey described reports that her missions agency asked her to submit on how she was doing. She never received responses to these reports. She lamented, "I'm sending you an e-mail and you are not responding. That's not support."

Jocelyn related an experience with a mentor whom she was assigned by her organization. Her mentor requested she write down some examples of things that had happened in her ministry. She said, "I did and sent it, and I am still waiting to hear a response from her. I don't even think she works at the organization anymore. I don't know what happened. I never, ever heard from her again; it was strange." Lack of follow-up communicates that the experiences or input of the young adult lack value to the mentor or organization.

Ana also described frustration with the lack of responsiveness from individuals in her missions agency. When she had a question that required their response, she said, "I had to contact them two or three times to respond to my request. I sent it to three people in the office, and I didn't hear anything back for three weeks." The poor communication by individuals in her organization resulted in her complete disengagement. "They don't even know that I am in the States right now; they don't know anything about me. I haven't done any training, I haven't read any books for them, and I haven't submitted any reports to them. They have never asked me why I haven't read the books; they never asked me why I am not doing the program, so for me, why am I going to do it if they don't even care? I am so saturated with work and things that I have to do." Young adults find it difficult to value the vision or goals of people who do not communicate that the young adult is valued.

Servant Leadership

Leaders and colleagues who demonstrate servant leadership qualities will find young adults much more inclined to follow them. Millennials appreciate leaders who value service, both to them and to others. Many young adults reported significant growth in their lives when leaders took the time to make them a priority and invest in their lives. Serving Millennials can require incredible humility and patience on the part of older leaders.

Millennials are in need of servant leaders in their lives who realize they are still developing and who earn the trust needed to challenge and encourage them. Leaders who are willing to serve young adults will have an opportunity to model important traits and help them develop into more competent, thoughtful, responsible leaders. These young leaders will be empowered and equipped to carry forth the vision of those servant leaders who have valued and developed them!

To Millennial Readers

Your generation chooses to respect and follow others based on vision, personality, and character. This approach provides great accountability to your leaders to be worthy of following. However, leaders with years of experience and who invested the significant time and energy that resulted in degrees, titles, and positions often possess valuable qualities and experience that may not always be readily visible to you. Take the time to observe your leaders. Understand the price they have paid to be where they are. Value them. Galatians 6:7 says that we will reap what we sow. If you desire to be a leader who receives respect, you must begin now by giving respect to those you follow. As a young leader, David gave respect to King Saul, a leader who definitely demonstrated unworthy characteristics. Today, David is known as one of the greatest leaders of the Bible. He is indeed a worthy example to follow as a young leader!

QUESTIONS FOR REFLECTION

1. To what extent does your church/ministry/organization possess a clearly articulated vision? Who participated in its development? Does everyone involved sense ownership of the vision? Why or why not?

2. Which do you value more: the success of your church/ministry/organization or the success of its people? How do you communicate your values?

3. Would others describe you as a servant leader? Why or why not?

CHAPTER 11

Fulfillment and Effectiveness in Role

Lindsey, a young woman serving in Asia, described the meaning she found working at a community organization. "Six months sounds like a long time, but when you are in another culture [and] learning a language, getting to know people doesn't happen right away. Now, I am enjoying it because I understand how the organization works, because I have relationships. The depth of my relationships is what is going to bring fruit." She explained, "I can help improve this organization; I am actually an asset, not just a volunteer trying to figure things out. It was neat to realize that, to find my niche and to have the relationships that I do with the girls who work here and with the other volunteers also." The sense of meaning and fulfillment she experienced in her role contributed to a commitment to stay. "It's been fun too, to be a part of a staff and to be committed for a while. I've really enjoyed it."

Millennials desire a job that holds meaning beyond simply making a living. Those who are making financial sacrifices to work in ministry positions especially want to know they are making a difference. While some young adults may need coaching in faithfully fulfilling the more mundane but necessary tasks in their roles, those hiring young adults can maximize the energy and insights of Millennials by understanding their abilities and passions and empowering them in areas of skill. Kris, a young youth pastor, explained the importance of empowering his generation by harnessing passion and fit. "We struggle to find ourselves really pouring into something. I think once we can find our niche, we really invest into it, but if we don't find that, then we just kind of hang back and really don't invest." The following section illustrates experiences that led to young leaders choosing either to invest or to become disillusioned in their roles.

Meaning and Fulfillment

In many cases, for young adults I interviewed, *meaning* emerged from the aspects of ministry that dealt directly with people in the specific ministry area for which they were hired. Sam, a youth pastor, explained that his favorite part of the job was working with young people. "I loved Wednesday nights. I loved the students."

Making a difference in people's lives resonates with Millennials in ministry. Jesse explained, "Every Wednesday night, I feel I'm connected with these students and I want to do more." He was energized by "just planting seeds in students" to take with them wherever they might go. "Maybe they are going to be working at corporations, and they're going to have access to people I'll never reach . . . or maybe they'll be teachers. I want to train other people to do great things." Jesse wanted to be a launching pad for others. "I would love nothing better than to hear students that were in my ministry say, 'I'm a construction worker and I've led ten people to Christ, and I just want to thank you.'"

Randy echoed a similar sentiment. "I think the thing that makes me the most happy is when I see a student who has graduated [from] our youth ministry and is still serving the Lord." Randy, understanding the hurdles many young people have to overcome, explained, "Knowing I had a major part in getting them to that point, that probably brings me more satisfaction than anything else." He contrasted that with "seeing the students that aren't serving God anymore," which he described as "pretty devastating."

Although many aspects of pastoring can be difficult, he said, "It crushes you to think about how much you poured into those students' lives and now they've rejected that. That's hard."

Young adults in ministry expressed dedication to the people in their churches and communities. Levi explained, "I absolutely loved my kids in the youth group. I still think about them a ton, and pray about them a ton. I just genuinely loved them and loved my interaction with them." This brought a sense of accomplishment for Levi: "I don't know if I was a good pastor in general, but I was a good youth pastor."

Success and fulfillment consistently corresponded with witnessing growth and changes in the lives of the people Millennials worked with in their ministries. Nina explained, "When I see growth . . . people developing and actually using their giftings . . . that makes me excited!" She appreciated seeing people step out of their comfort zones and be challenged. "You are like, oh my word, this is so good for them as a person! They are trusting God. It's just really neat." She especially loved getting her leaders all together in a room and asking, "What is God doing?"

Crystal also reported fulfillment in "just seeing lives changed." She told a story of one couple who came and gave their hearts to God: "[They] got involved really quickly and just really understood, 'If I'm going to follow Christ, I'm going to do it with everything I have.' It's true transformation, and I think that is the most rewarding thing to see." She enjoyed seeing people who had a genuine faith. "It is real passion, [people] saying, 'I don't want to do things like this because look what God's saved me from— look what God's done in my life!' And so, it's . . . just incredible to see people really changed."

Some participants enjoyed seeing their efforts effect change in the places where they were serving. Nina explained, "I think seeing progress in things makes me really excited. Seeing changes for the positive." Another young leader said, "There were so many times of great success. I mean, worship at that place was totally different when I went there. There were some times of awesome freedom, and different things were huge success stories for that church."

For some participants, the process of finding meaning was a journey and required effort in the midst of challenges or uncertainty. Gavin explained, "The thing that kept me going was, I knew there were leaders [whom] I was ministering to and who came every week looking forward to me coming in, just saying hi to them." He emphasized, "Find that aspect of the ministry and pour yourself into that because that's what keeps you going. . . . Find things that energize you, the reasons you are in ministry . . . even if it is not part of your job description."

Dana acknowledged, "Even though it's difficult and even though it's challenging, and even though I don't know what I am doing most of the time, there's this deep part of me being fulfilled and confirmed on a regular basis." Kris believed this fulfillment occurs when young adults finds those elements of ministry they would do without a paycheck. Empowering Millennials in this discovery produces meaning in their work for years to come.

Expectations and Responsibilities

Expectations can play an important role in young adult effectiveness and satisfaction in ministry roles. Julie, a young missionary, explained, "It is hard to know what to expect. My leader asked me the other day, 'Is what we do everything the missions agency said it was going to be?' And I said, 'Yes, I feel like we are doing what I was told.'"

Millennials have had the Internet at their fingertips since high school, if not since childhood. In a matter of seconds, they can find the menu of a favorite restaurant, the time it takes to get to a friend's house, or every degree and extracurricular program available at colleges of interest. Such access to information often means they aren't accustomed to surprises! Thus, changing or unmet expectations in ministry positions are often disorienting. Organizations or leaders hiring young adults for roles or situations where expectations and responsibilities are unclear need to be honest and communicate this up-front.

Calli wished her missions agency had communicated the reality of limited ministry opportunities on the field from the beginning.

"I was told I could do anything, so that was just another miscommunication where if I had known from the beginning, it would have been fine." She explained how difficult it was to arrive in a new country and find the situation very different than what had been described to her. "I think it would have been beneficial to understand the vision and goals for the ministry that they were sending us into."

Study participants described frequent encounters with unexpected responsibilities once in their ministry positions. If these did not fit with their skills or heart and passion, the result was often anxiety or frustration. For some, the new responsibilities proved an exciting challenge, but this was more likely the case when accompanied by supportive and invested leadership. Dana explained, after a year in her position, "I don't have a job description yet; we're still working on one." However, when she encountered something unfamiliar, her pastors encouraged her, "Dana, this isn't a scary thing." She explained how they walked her through the situation and showed her how to be effective. Others were often left to figure out the role on their own.

Levi confessed, "I had no idea what to expect. I had really only preached twice before. I didn't have any idea what I was doing." He described reading a book left by his predecessor. "I just read and did everything that book told me to do." Besides receiving little guidance in his new responsibilities, he found many things added to his job that no one had communicated when he interviewed. "There were a lot of things that were not communicated up-front, so then it was just the expectation I would learn how to do it."

When Sam entered his first ministry role, he made a big transition from another full-time job outside of church. "I finished that job, and the next week I started as youth pastor. I'm in my office, I'm sitting there thinking, 'Here you go, here's the youth ministry, have fun.'" It took him a couple of months to figure out the specific tasks in his new role. While there, he also acquired additional tasks. He explained, "I was the youth pastor, and then playing on the worship team—all while having the expectation to just do young adult ministry, without a lot of guidance, without a lot of ministry accountability." The support he needed to feel effective was lacking.

In Gavin's experience, his job responsibilities changed after he was hired. "It was different than what was initially advertised. My job, little by little, became less about small groups and more about other events. The position slowly became something different than what it was advertised as." When changes to responsibilities occurred without communication and support from leaders, participants often felt ineffective. In many cases, their passions and skills did not match the additional duties and requirements, compounding their frustration.

In some cases, not only the young adult, but parents or other significant individuals have expectations regarding new roles the young adult is pursuing. Lindsey explained, "I am a detail-oriented person. I want to know things thoroughly before I step into them. All of our parents were asking questions too, so they would feel more safe, and I was asking a lot of questions. We were getting mixed answers. I felt like sometimes asking questions was discouraged, or it was expected we would figure things out when we got there. They weren't thorough and didn't really answer our questions, and I didn't really feel prepared going into it." Not every young adult needs to know what they are walking into, but most will have questions, and honest responses to those questions can help alleviate future tension and ineffectiveness in the ministry team.

Most young ministers desperately want to please those who hire them and meet the expectations of new teammates and leaders. When expectations of them are unclear, this can produce insecurity and anxiety. Connie explained, "We weren't really given orientation. Our team leader was very, very hands-off. They never met about any team stuff or explained what they expected from us, how we could be helpful to them. Getting there and not knowing how we fit in with the people who were already there was confusing. I thought we would be working with them, but that's not really what happened."

Another young woman shared her experience of arriving at her ministry site for the launch meeting. "There were a lot of things talked about in that meeting, rules and plans, that were different from anything I knew." Instead of being allowed to start her internship shortly after arriving, as had been communicated, she discovered she would be doing nine months of cultural and language training before beginning her internship. "It felt like things were constantly changing. Our leader over the summer had told me we were going to be focusing on a drop-in center and to tell all of my supporters about the drop-in center, so I did, and then I got to the field and the team there said, 'What are you talking about? We're nowhere near doing that.' I just didn't know that was how it was going to be." When unclear expectations hinder young adults' ability to effectively serve their teams, leaders, and supporters, or to use their gifts and skills, they can quickly become discouraged.

Personalities, Gifts, and Passions

Kris reflected on attitudes regarding personalities, gifts, and passions in his generation. "It's very trendy right now to categorize yourself as a certain personality type. A lot of people use that as a crutch and they say, 'I can't perform this job function because that's not my personality; it's deterring my natural gifts.'" While some use their personality type or lack of skills in a particular area as an excuse for ineffectiveness, a good fit between a role and an individual's gifts and passions can maximize that person's effectiveness and retention in ministry.

Sean affirmed the importance of people being in a place where they fit: "You need different people, but they have to be in the right places." In describing her application for a ministry position, Julie said, "As they started to talk about it, I began to realize that the whole program just wasn't set up for my personality and what I am good at doing. I didn't feel like I would be thriving there. Even my mom said, 'When you told me about it, that didn't really sound like you.' So, I decided, that wasn't what I was going to do."

Some young adults I interviewed found it disconcerting when their personalities or passions did not coalesce with their positions. Jesse said of his church, "It was always very creative. So, whether it was a creative sermon or a creative type of worship experience, it was a very fast-paced youth ministry, a very fast-paced church in general." He told his pastor, "I feel like the church is going 300 miles per hour and I am going 150 miles per hour, and this is as fast as I can go, and yet I am still falling faster and faster behind." In working with his colleagues at the church, he said, "[I] felt like all these guys were way more creative than me. So, for me to have top-notch, great-quality stuff all the time, [it] put pressure on me."

Jesse finally determined he could not stay at that church. "I think God has gifted me in certain areas," he said, but they were not being maximized in his position. He revealed his passion for future youth ministry opportunities. "I know I'm very much a shepherd, and relationships are a big part of the youth ministry. It's not going to be an event-driven type of youth ministry; it will be a lot more [about] relationships."

Early ministry positions sometimes provided opportunities for young adults to learn what was important to them and how they wanted to minister. Sam explained, "That first church, my first job was a huge refining process. It's very valuable to me, that time, but it wasn't great; it wasn't a good fit." Although he learned a lot, he admitted, "It didn't turn out to be a great fit for me and my personality, for my style and my vision." Sam contrasted that experience in his first position with his new role in a different setting. "It's an environment where I'm working in my strengths, I'm being challenged. I'm working in a driven environment, and I'm working in a healthy environment." He explained, "We always have to do things we're not good at, things we don't like to do; that's just the reality of life. But when you're doing that with the majority of your time, it can be hard."

Those who did utilize their gifts and passions regularly found the experience very fulfilling. Kris described being in a position where he was able to engage in activities he really enjoyed. Being able to implement his personal passions into his work was meaningful. He drew on that experience in defining good leadership: "I think it is recognizing people's strengths and abilities and being able to then plug them in where they'll be most successful."

Other participants echoed the importance of recognizing and empowering people in their gifts. Kate explained, "I believe everyone has a gift; everyone has lots of gifts." She emphasized empowering others by placing them in situations where they would be most effective and would benefit most from the experience. Dana emphasized valuing all gifts and ensuring that people do not feel "like they have to look a certain way or have a certain gift." She expressed appreciation for her pastors' ability to affirm others. "God has given them this ability to see the gifts God has given you. In everyday interactions, they can see specific things God has put there and call them out. They help to foster that and help you grow." Dana went on to describe her development as a young minister: "God has just blessed me so abundantly by giving me the opportunity to work here. They've deposited so much into me, things to be a church leader." Investing in the growth of Millennials as they discover and practice their gifts and passions can contribute to a life of meaningful service.

To Millennial Readers

While we all work most effectively when our jobs are fulfilling and meaningful, mature leaders understand that seasons of learning, adapting, and remaining faithful through change and unexpected developments are necessary and unavoidable. How do you remain motivated when you feel unfulfilled? Think of a time when circumstances unfolded differently than what someone communicated to you or what you expected. How did you respond? How would you respond in the future? Think about the leadership skills that will help you remain effective through the many changes and unexpected developments of long-term ministry. Identify someone who is strong in these areas. Ask him or her to mentor you and hold you accountable as you grow in your leadership abilities.

QUESTIONS FOR REFLECTION

1. To what extent does your church/ministry/organization clearly communicate job expectations and responsibilities prior to hiring new staff members?

2. What efforts are made to understand the personalities and gifts of individuals on your team and utilize these effectively?

3. How are changes to job responsibilities or organizational goals communicated to ensure understanding and buy-in?

PART IV

Practical Applications

CHAPTER 12

A Word to Millennials

Genesis 37 tells the story of young Joseph. The life of Joseph, though lived in ancient times, presents encouragement for the Millennial generation in the United States. Like many Millennials today, Joseph enjoyed loving parental involvement in his life. The Scriptures tell us Joseph's father, Jacob, loved him more than any of his brothers. His father gave him preferential treatment, making him an ornate robe indicating he was special. Verses 5 through 11 describe Joseph's dreams, the interpretations of which implied he had been promoted to a place of prominence while his family bowed down to him. This produced intergenerational conflict with his father and brothers, as his attitude appeared confident, arrogant, and entitled.

While we cannot know the intentions of Joseph's heart as a young man, his boldness in sharing self-promoting dreams, and his brothers' response to him, indicate a potential lack of humility and sensitivity to others. Sociologists may have diagnosed Joseph with the same narcissism or desire for promotion they identify in young adults today. Nonetheless, his dreams were accurate, even prophetic. Joseph was special. I believe the same is true of Millennials. The messages spoken over you as being special and gifted are true. However, like Joseph, your path to the fulfillment of those prophetic messages may be long and arduous. The desire instilled by our culture for instantaneous and easy results could be your undoing. Many of your generation will fail to reach the destiny God has for them because they lack Joseph's faith, commitment, and willingness to learn and sacrifice.

Joseph's brothers, exasperated by his seeming arrogance, seized an opportunity to sell him as a slave. For many years, Joseph lived as a slave and prisoner, subject to the jealousy, lies, and unfaithfulness of those around him. His response to difficult circumstances and unfair treatment forged his character and revealed his readiness to serve in the role God had ordained for him. He made a choice in his trials to remain faithful to God, to others, and to the tasks he was given. The lessons learned during that difficult time proved essential to his leadership preparation. He did indeed rise to a position of prominence as depicted in the dreams of his youth. In that position, his discernment, character, and leadership skills served to preserve a nation and his own family through a desperate time.

I believe the Holy Spirit desires to use this generation to discern God's will and competently lead the church through the season to come. However, preparation for this role may require long years of refining and training for the days ahead. Your response to what may feel like slave shackles or a prison cell will determine the fulfillment of your destiny.

As I interviewed Millennials serving in ministry roles around the globe, I witnessed the struggles and trials many are facing and overcoming. I asked some of them to share what they have learned. Sam reflected on his first position as a youth pastor.

> I learned a lot about myself, as a pastor and as a leader of people. It was hard because I went there based on the potential of the church, thinking I could come in and do so many great things. Then I realized I could only do so much. The bright-eyed, bushy-tailed, head-in-the-clouds, so-excited perspective came smacking down to reality, and that was hard. I came out of college thinking I could just take on the world, and I was just awesome, and I went to this church and got humbled like crazy and taken back to reality.

Sam also emphasized the importance of learning about hard work and professionalism. "Talent will get you places; hard work will keep you there. Don't rely on your talents."

Dana also referenced the transition from idealism to reality in her first ministry position. "God is bringing me through a season of showing me I don't know everything. I think I came into college thinking I pretty much knew everything." Once in her first ministry role, she experienced a period of really learning what it meant to be a pastor. She admitted, "I love it. It's fun, as much as it's challenging. Every week I am learning something new about myself or about the people I love or about God or about what it means to do church." She explained learning about the value of vulnerability and authenticity in pastoring or "shepherding." Referring to her senior pastors, she said, "I will model them, not just because it is them, but because I believe they are really living out the way Jesus wants us to live in every part of our lives. They've earned a special place in my heart." After delineating other lessons, including the values of listening, appreciating the ideas of others, and supporting the vision of her leader, Dana took a long, reflective pause and stated, "And, I've learned how to pray!"

Many young adults learned from leaders they respected. Jesse explained modeling his own ministry after his mentors.

> I sat in their offices and picked their brains or just talked about life. I'd share what was going on in my life and they would come down on me and say, "You're being an idiot right now." I feel like I got a wealth of knowledge because I surrounded myself with great people. That was a huge win for me.

Upon reflecting on advice he would give to someone preparing for ministry, Jesse said, "I would say, 'Find a mentor!' I definitely needed a mentor badly, and not necessarily just for youth ministry, but for life in general."

For those without mentors or supportive leaders, lessons often came through experience or a personal spiritual journey. Kate explained, "Probably the biggest thing I learned was the difference between serving the church and serving God. Sometimes that is the same thing and sometimes it is very different." She realized, "When it comes down to it, I want to be able to say I served God the whole time." She also talked about her relationship with God and stressed the importance of recognizing its essence: "It's a relationship with a Person, a real person who has something to say about your life. It's an adventure with [God]. Spending time in a thankless type of role is worth it, because you develop depth with the Lord."

Being humble and allowing God to teach you do not necessarily mean remaining in an abusive or dysfunctional situation. Many young leaders burn out because of unwise choices or lack of discernment. Several young adults referred to important aspects of looking for and accepting a ministry position. Levi said, "I think asking more specific questions in the interview process is so valuable." He spoke of the pressure on many young graduates to find a job, and cautioned against the attitude of viewing one's first position as simply a stepping stone. "I think there's that pull towards wanting something, and I think a lot of people have the expectation, 'This isn't where I am going to end up, this is just the first step.'" He warned of the danger in this approach. "There's more at stake. You can get pretty roughed up in a year or two. I would say, ask a lot of questions, and then if it is possible to interact with people from the church, ask candid questions."

Jon referred to being careful and thorough in the application process as well. "Find the right fit; find the right place." He elaborated, "[I would do] the research to know I'm going into someplace healthy, where I will grow as a leader, I will be supported, I will be nurtured, and I will be able to expand on what God's calling me to do." Carly echoed this advice. "When you go [to interview], know the right questions to ask about the health of the church. Do your research."

Gavin urged those going into ministry to seek divine direction. "If it's from God, do it, but don't do it if it is not from God, because it will destroy your life." He explained, "[Ministry is] not like a job where you can just go and make money for a couple of years and leave it and not care about whether the business is good or bad or if you helped it or not." Gavin summed up the reflections of many young leaders regarding lessons learned in ministry when he stated, "The church is all about people, so you need to make sure it is God [leading you]."

Millennials are called to lead in a unique period of history. Within the next few decades, the church could fulfill the Great Commission of taking the gospel to every tribe, nation, and tongue. This generation has a unique opportunity to participate in the fulfillment of centuries of faithful investment and service by believers worldwide. With great privilege come great responsibility, sacrifice, and joy. Will Millennials respond to God's calling on their generation and rise to the challenge?

CHAPTER 13

A Word to Leaders of Millennials

"After three years of working with my missions agency, I now understand why the older leaders feel the way they do. I can identify with them and their frustrations as younger leaders come to work on our team." As a Millennial, Kelli had come to identify with older leaders regarding her generation. She observed the attitudes and behaviors of young leaders that threatened and disrupted the harmony and effectiveness of teams and systems developed by hard-working individuals over months and years of faithful service. However, Kelli did not reach that realization, or remain in the organization as a contributing member, by chance. She was hired by a mature leader who committed to coaching and mentoring her, supporting her when she was the new leader lacking awareness and understanding. Furthermore, her leader understood the benefit of her perspective and talents, and he empowered her, ultimately benefiting the organization with the energy and ideas she brought. Young leaders desperately need senior leaders and mentors like Kelli had in her first ministry role. Finding them, however, can prove challenging.

Ministry today looks very different than it did when many leaders of Millennials began serving. Different experiences make it difficult at times to comprehend the perspectives and expectations of young adults. Twenty years ago, the Internet, e-mail, instant messaging, video conferencing, and cell phones were in their infancy or did not exist. If you moved to a foreign country or far from home, you likely communicated with family infrequently or not at all. Often, no one provided support or supervision as you endeavored to begin new ministries, plant fledgling churches, or pioneer new missions endeavors. Perhaps you started in ministry with little training or preparation and had to rely on God's guidance and your own initiative to learn. After many years of faithful service, endless sacrifice, and hard work, you may now find yourself in a position of supervising young adults who seem self-centered and uncommitted. They may expect others to give them the things older generations have had to work to obtain. Their need for constant feedback and meaningful relationships requires extensive time and energy, and they seem unwilling to make the sacrifices of time and commitment, personal preferences, or hard work that most successful leaders in your churches or organizations have made.

The challenges of intergenerational leadership make it easy to forget that each generation faces unique struggles. Young adults today grew up witnessing and experiencing cultural, familial, and ideological factors some older adults have not had to confront. Effective leadership of Millennials requires the emotional intelligence to acknowledge that while they may not view or respond to opportunities and experiences the way Silents, Boomers, and even Xers may prefer, they will lead through circumstances and challenges we may never see or understand.

Failure to invest in Millennials and prepare them for effective and enduring leadership deprives the kingdom of God of leaders desperately needed to guide churches and organizations through tumultuous times ahead. Furthermore, it leaves the future of our vision and ministry in peril when current leaders are unable to continue their work. Cultural and generational experts Chip Espinoza,

Mick Ukleja, and Craig Rusch explain the dilemma for organizations as many executives plan to retire. "The people in the second, third, and fourth positions are also Baby Boomers, and they're going to be retiring, too. Long story short, an organization's future vitality is dependent on its ability to attract, retain, motivate, and develop Millennials."[1] So, how do we respond to the current challenges of intergenerational leadership?

Dealing with the pressures inherent in leadership positions, some find it easy to discount, disregard, or even ignore young leaders who require more time, energy, and attention than seems reasonable. We become susceptible to the belief that it is not worth investing in their lives or futures. Some leaders even try to avoid hiring Millennials because of the complications they bring. A temptation in leadership is to focus on what leadership expert Steven Covey termed the *urgent*, rather than the *important*. "Urgent matters are usually visible. They press on us; they insist on action."[2]

Often, important matters are not as urgent and require more initiative. The important requires action, not just reaction. Older generations often look at young employees and staff for what they can contribute right now to "our" pressing priorities. How do they serve *our* church, *our* organization, *our* team or project? If their contributions to what we are doing right now do not seem to justify the time and effort required to coach, mentor, teach, correct, and encourage them, then we do not make the effort. We can fail to see young leaders as an investment into the future of God's kingdom. While the deposits we make into a young leader may not generate the results we desire right now, they do represent the legacy we will leave behind.

Discernment and wisdom must guide our decisions regarding what is important. One young leader I talked to worked at several churches where he witnessed leaders hiring and investing in his peers who never intended to serve in ministry. He encouraged leaders, "Hire people who want to go into ministry full-time." He saw many of his young colleagues serving for a few years and then leaving ministry because it was a fun job but they lacked calling. He believed pastors and leaders "are in a prime position to be able to equip and mentor and raise up the next leaders." However, when today's leaders hire people based on availability or excitement alone, rather than helping them to understand their call and to respond accordingly, we often miss opportunities to teach future leaders about ministry.

A common trap for leaders, churches, or organizations in responding to Millennials is to adopt an extreme approach. Some strive to adapt fully to the needs, desires, even whims of the younger generation. This often results from a desire to be trendy, innovative, or liked by young staff, and these leaders tend to reflect parenting styles that seek to befriend rather than teach or lead younger generations. Another approach refuses to change or adapt to the needs of younger members or leaders. Steeped in tradition, new and different methods or perspectives present a threat to either the comfort or power of those in authority. The right balance exists somewhere in between.

As tradition and youth collide, a common point of tension often arises over who or what must adapt. In their book, *Managing the Millennials,* Espinoza, Ukleja, and Rusch contend, "The people with the most responsibility have to adapt first. It may sound cliché, but by setting an example, managers will create an environment in which the less mature will adapt." Leaders need to recognize "adapting does not mean acquiescing to the whims of an individual or generation."[3] It does require meeting young adults where they are, and developing the trust, support, and expectations needed to enable growth and development beyond that point. To leave them where they are is to fail in our responsibility to train and empower them for future leadership roles.

Some of the most effective models for developing and leading young adults include both mentors and coaches. As discussed earlier, Millennials value meaningful relationships with leaders. They need feedback, affirmation, and support. Mentors can provide this safety net for young adults as they develop and grow. However, Millennials also need help to overcome the constraints of their generation. This requires loving accountability, guidance, and realistic and challenging expectations and goals. A good coach knows how to push players to be their best, even when the process feels strenuous. Environments or leaders that provide both elements, supporting and pushing, will see the greatest success in fostering effective leadership for the future.

Leading through this season of intense generational diversity requires courage, discernment, and humility. Few periods in history have experienced the rapid change occurring in our culture today. While we must study and observe in order to understand the dynamics around us, prayer and flexibility are essential to our role. I admire you for taking on the challenge of being an engaged and courageous intergenerational leader.

NOTES

1. Chip Espinoza, Mick Ukleja, and Craig Rusch, *Managing the Millennials: Discover the Core Competencies for Managing Today's Workforce* (Hoboken, NJ: John Wiley & Sons Inc., 2010), 8.

2. Stephen R. Covey, *The 7 Habits of Highly Effective People: Powerful Lessons in Personal Change* (New York: Simon & Schuster, 1989), 150–51.

3. Espinoza, Ukleja, and Rusch, 25.

CHAPTER 14

Putting It into Practice

Is your church or organization conducive to fostering effective intergenerational teams and collaboration? Are you proactively hiring and retaining individuals from diverse generations on your ministry team? Where are you extremely successful in understanding young leaders? Where could you use some help?

While this book provides an overview of the generational traits, values, and needs of Millennials in ministry, implementing effective strategies to engage them can be challenging. This chapter offers simple assessments for you to use to determine practical application of the material covered in the previous chapters. These tools are meant to be used in the context of team discussion, soliciting feedback from members of various generational cohorts. Different methods may be needed to accommodate the various needs and perspectives in your organization. A one-size-fits-all approach does not work anymore. Getting feedback and ownership from representatives of every group in your organization will help you determine the best strategies for maximizing the effectiveness of your intergenerational team.

Generational Traits

Diverse generational traits exist in the workplace today. Most churches and organizations favor the preferences and perspectives of Boomers, and sometimes Xers or Silents. Few accommodate the characteristics Millennials bring with them into the workplace, until employee turnover or team conflict demand they do so. Let's review some of the key traits and important practices to consider as we assess to what extent your ministry is Millennial-friendly.

Special

Millennials need to know they are valued. They want to be known and appreciated for the gifts and uniqueness they bring to a team or organization. Understanding the personalities, strengths, and interests of young staff members and affirming those qualities communicates your personal investment in their lives.

Give Millennials specific, regular, and spontaneous feedback! Eliminate formal annual performance reviews, which communicate that feedback is perfunctory. Instead, give constructive feedback upon completion of projects or assignments, in regular mentoring or coaching sessions, or spontaneously stop by their office or drop them an e-mail. Just be sure it occurs often. Provide accountability and guidance as needed, but also affirm why they are important to the ministry! When possible, recognize and affirm all staff publicly for their contributions. While we all perform best when appreciated, Millennials seldom tolerate being underappreciated!

Sheltered

The protection and guidance most Millennials received from adults in their lives as they grew up may limit their ability to manage stress and employ effective time-management and problem-solving skills. Many seem idealistic or naïve, in part because of parents shielding them from life's realities or struggles. Young adults entering ministry positions need a balance of support, to keep them from faltering, and strategic development that enables them to handle the pressures of ministry and leadership.

Provide hands-on training for Millennials in new positions, and coach new staff members on specific expectations for managing time and resources. Ensure relational support as they adjust to the culture of your organization. Do not exclude them from difficult decisions or challenging situations because they seem immature or inexperienced. Rather, use these opportunities to expose them to real-life situations and the complex nature of problem-solving. Model healthy skills they will need in the future. Take time to debrief what they observed and learned, addressing areas for potential development in a constructive manner.

Collaborative

Our education system and society placed great emphasis on teamwork and collaboration as Millennials grew up. As a result, they greatly value collaboration, though their definition sometimes lacks understanding of healthy conflict or results in stalemates when each person wants his or her own preferences considered. Authentic collaboration, however, provides many benefits to organizations and teams, including creative solutions, ownership of decisions and vision by many, and the elimination of bureaucratic silos and divisions.

Provide both formal and informal opportunities for staff to get to know one another. This can be as simple as having someone share a personal testimony at the beginning of each staff meeting, providing a coffee station to facilitate water cooler conversation, or inviting staff over to your home to connect in a personal setting. As individuals get to know each other and develop trust, teamwork and collaboration will improve.

Connected

Millennials are digital natives. The immediacy and connectivity of the digital world are part of who they are. For those of us who had to learn how to use technology, it is hard to understand Millennials' intuitiveness in utilizing technological tools to interact with others. Rather than prohibiting access to social media or mobile devices, establish guidelines and expectations that facilitate young adults' need to connect while also minimizing distractions and frustration for older generations or bosses. Furthermore, as you seek to connect with Millennials, utilize the tools that they are comfortable using. They can help your organization remain up-to-date in a digital age!

Work/Life Balance

Millennials approach work with a focus on protecting their priorities, especially priorities related to taking care of themselves and their families. They work to live. This creates conflict in ministry settings where many older leaders have poured themselves out for the work and expect others to do the same. While some of the Millennial approach to work/life balance emerges from selfishness, it also results from watching many older adults burn out or sacrifice relationships, health, and personal growth for ministry interests.

Encourage learning from the various generational perspectives in your organization. Young adults need to appreciate the work ethic of older generations. Explain why hard work is important and encourage mentorship in this regard. At the same time, affirm Millennials' concern for healthy boundaries between home and work. Enforce adequate personal time and rest for all staff. The overall well-being and effectiveness of your entire team and organization will benefit.

Growth and Advancement

The days of working in one profession (often for the same organization) for thirty years are gone. The rapid evolution of new technologies, emerging models of ministry, and globalization ensure that jobs today will disappear or look very different in even five or ten years. Most college degrees provide only a foundation for building upon; continuing education provides the skills, qualifications, and knowledge individuals will need for jobs yet to emerge. Young adults understand the need for constant growth and advancement to remain competitive in a difficult job market. They value roles and opportunities that build their résumé.

Be sure to provide opportunities for growth and mobility that permit gaining new skills and preparing for future roles. This might include offering special courses, facilitating learning communities, diversifying job experiences, or adding new positions and titles young adults can strive to achieve. Take advantage of Millennials' comfort with technology to explore opportunities for vocational development through webinars, online courses, and other virtual trainings.

Leadership and Authority

Millennials decide whom they value as leaders and whose authority they feel compelled to respect. They expect competence, effectiveness, authenticity, and relationship from those they follow. Leaders who demonstrate they value the input and contributions of young adults will gain their respect.

Promote opportunities for honest interaction with senior leaders. Establish an open-door policy for staff to meet with leaders. Facilitate regular one-on-one meetings or discussion groups with leaders. Solicit feedback from staff regularly and address concerns or suggestions promptly. In large or international agencies, leaders can demonstrate approachability by facilitating online forums and by meeting in person with young leaders during orientation or other gatherings.

Technology and Communication

Effective communication strategies are essential for healthy intergenerational teams. The efficiency of technology creates expectations regarding communication. Develop policies for your team or organization regarding expected response times to e-mails, text messages, or other communications.

I highly recommend an initial acknowledgment of messages received within 48 hours. If a full response will take longer than that, give the expected time frame and be sure to respond as quickly as you can. When travel or vacation might affect your availability, clearly communicate when individuals can expect to hear from you. Some older leaders may find the communication of young colleagues frustrating as it can seem brief, sloppy, or untactful as a result of the many informal and immediate communication tools they utilize. When needed, require supervisors to review important communication from young leaders and to give feedback before it goes out. Provide training for all parties to understand the different perspectives on communication and expectations within your team or organization.

Compensation and Benefits

Young adults want to receive fair compensation because it communicates value and appreciation of their contributions. However, many other factors affect job satisfaction. Ministry roles often cannot pay large salaries, but they can offer other benefits such as personal and professional mentoring and coaching, meaningful work opportunities, flexibility in work schedules, unique learning opportunities, and a sense of team and belonging. Ministries and teams that maximize the opportunities that ministry contexts provide to meet Millennial needs and expectations greatly increase the potential of retaining young leaders longer and influencing them for future ministry roles.

In the remainder of this chapter we will review these values and needs of the emerging generation of leaders. But first, I invite you to complete the assessment at right to determine the extent to which your team or organization acknowledges and responds to the Millennial characteristics discussed above. Have others on your team, including Millennials, complete it as well. Determine areas of needed growth or disparity of perspective. Facilitate discussion and develop goals that will help you move toward more effective intergenerational interactions.

Generational Values

In Part II of this book, we discussed the Millennial values of ministry-as-family versus ministry-as-business. While ministry ideally incorporates the love, sacrifice, commitment, and discipline of a healthy family, it also requires the wise stewardship practices of an effective business. On intergenerational ministry teams these values often compete, rather than coexisting in a complementary way.

CHAPTER 14, FIGURE 1: **Assessment of Millennial-Friendly Practices**

Millennial Trait	Agree (4)	Somewhat Agree (3)	Somewhat Disagree (2)	Disagree (1)	Not Applicable
1. Special: Individuals receive regular, specific feedback and affirmation.					
2. Sheltered: One-on-one mentoring or job skills coaching are available or required for new staff.					
3. Collaborative: Staff work together regularly on projects and initiatives.					
4. Collaborative: Intentional efforts are made to facilitate healthy relationships among team members.					
5. Connected: Ongoing efforts exist for improving the ministry's web and social media presence.					
6. Work/Life Balance: Work schedules allow for flexibility and an acceptable amount of personal time.					
7. Growth/Advancement: Staff receive funds and/or opportunities for personal growth, development, and advancement.					
8. Leadership/Authority: Staff have regular access to leadership throughout the organization.					
9. Communication: Clear policies or training exist regarding expectations for quality communication and effective response time.					
10. Compensation: Staff feel that compensation and benefits represent the value they contribute to the team/organization.					
TOTAL (add totals for each column)		+	+	+	= (add 4 points to total for every item marked N/A)

Millennial-Friendly Rating:
37–40: Great! Your team or organization is Millennial-friendly!
33–36: Good! You recognize Millennial needs and are working to respond to them!
30–32: Okay! Continue to work on identifying areas for change and improvement!
Under 30: Help! Time to invest serious focus and energy to address becoming an effective intergenerational team/organization!

To better understand the culture of your ministry, take a moment to consider the aspects of your team or organization that reflect family values versus business principles. Create a chart with two columns, one for "Like a Family" and one for "Like a Business," and use it to record whatever comes to mind. Ask members of your staff or team to do the same. As a group, discuss the values most evident in your ministry and identify areas of imbalance or needed change. Your organizational culture should reflect values of every generation you hope to attract and retain. A church or agency desiring to attract young people but functioning primarily as a business will see little success.

Generational Needs and Expectations

Part III of this book discussed generational needs and expectations as related to ministry calling, vital relationships, communication of vision and value, and fulfillment and effectiveness in ministry roles. While these topics were addressed in regard to Millennials, they are likely needs of every generation represented on your team. How these needs are met may differ among age groups, but effective leaders find ways to address them and create a healthy ministry environment where individuals and teams thrive.

The questions at right can facilitate team discussion and help develop action steps around generational needs and expectations. Discuss them in an extended staff development setting, or address one or two at a time in regular staff meetings or trainings. Find the solutions that work best in your intergenerational ministry setting!

My hope in writing, training, and coaching on the topic of Millennials in ministry is to equip the body of Christ to serve effectively during this critical time in history. I pray that the information presented here has empowered you to engage every generation as you labor to advance the kingdom of God. Please let me know how I can serve you with strategic training, coaching, or consulting to maximize the intergenerational effectiveness of your ministry or organization! Visit my website at www.leadingtomorrow.org or send me an e-mail at jolene@leadingtomorrow.org.

CHAPTER 14, FIGURE 2: **Assessment of Needs and Expectations on Intergenerational Teams**

Discussion Point	How are we doing?	How can we improve?
1. Calling: How many leaders or team members know the history of how other individuals were led or called into ministry?		
2. Calling: How is ministry calling recognized and developed on our team/ministry?		
3. Relationships: How accessible are leaders to staff/team members?		
4. Relationships: To what extent are personal relationships/friendships encouraged on our ministry team?		
5. Relationships: How are mentoring or coaching relationships fostered or developed?		
6. Relationships: What causes team members stress when interacting with members from other generations?		
7. Vision: How do different members of our ministry team understand the overall vision?		
8. Value: How do leaders communicate the value individuals bring to the ministry?		
9. Fulfillment: What provides fulfillment for different individuals on our team?		
10. Effectiveness: How are expectations for staff/team members communicated? How effective are these communication methods?		
11. Effectiveness: To what extent is there understanding and utilization of individual personalities, talents, and spiritual gifts on our ministry team?		